Microsoft Office 2013 Keyboard Shortcuts

For Windows

By

U. C-Abel Books.

All Rights Reserved

First Edition: 2016

Contents At A Glance

Table of Contents

CHAPTER 11: Keyboard Shortcuts In PowerPoint 2013.

CHAPTER 12: Keyboard Shortcuts In Visio 2013.

Customer's Page.

Download Our Free EBooks Today.

Other Books By This Publisher.

Acknowledgement.

U. C-Abel Books will not take all the credits for Microsoft Office 2013 keyboard shortcuts listed in this book, but shares it with Microsoft Corporation as some of the shortcut keys came from them and are "used with permission from Microsoft".

Dedication

This book is dedicated to computer users and lovers of
keyboard shortcuts all over the world.

Introduction.

We enjoy using shortcut keys because they set us on a high plane that astonishes people around us when we work with them. As wonderful shortcuts users, the worst eyesore we witness in computing is to see somebody sluggishly struggling to execute a task through mouse usage when in actual sense shortcuts will help save that person the overall time. Most people have asked us to help them with a list of shortcut keys that can make them work as smartly as we do and that drove us into research to broaden our knowledge and truly help them as they demanded, that is the reason for the existence of this book. It is a great tool for lovers of shortcuts, and those who want to join the group.

Most times, the things we love don't come by easily. It is our love for keyboard shortcuts that made us to bear long sleepless nights like owls, just to make sure we get the best out of it, and it is the best we got that we are sharing with you in this book. You cannot be the same at computing after reading this book. The time you entrusted to our care is an expensive possession and we promise not to mess it up.

Thank you.

What to Know Before You Begin.

General Notes.

1. It is important to note that when using shortcuts to perform any command, you should make sure the target area is active, if not, you may get a wrong result. Example, if you want to highlight all texts, you must make sure the text field is active and if an object, make sure the object area is active. The active area is always known by the location where the cursor of your computer blinks.

2. Most of the keyboard shortcuts you will see in this book refer to the U.S. keyboard layout. Keys for other layouts might not correspond exactly to the keys on a U.S. keyboard.

3. The plus (+) signs that come in the middle of keyboard shortcuts simply mean the keys are meant to be combined or held down together not to be added as one of the shortcut keys. In a case where plus sign is needed; it will be duplicated (++).

4. For keyboard shortcuts in which you press one key immediately followed by another key, the keys are separated by a comma (,).

5. It is also important to note that the shortcut keys listed in this book are for Microsoft Office 2013.

Microsoft Lync 2013.

Use the keyboard shortcuts listed for Lync 2013 in this book no matter which window has the focus.

The list of keyboard shortcuts in this book for Lync 2013 applies to: Lync 2013 for Office 365, Skype for Business, Lync 2013 for Office 365 operated by 21Vianet, Lync Basic 2013, Lync 2013.

Some features might not be available for your account. We've indicated these.

Microsoft PowerPoint 2013.
This topic assumes that JAWS users have turned off the Virtual Ribbon Menu feature.

The list of keyboard shortcuts in this book for PowerPoint 2013 applies to: Project Standard 2013, Project Professional 2013.

Microsoft Project 2013.
The list of keyboard shortcuts in this book for Project 2013 applies to: Project Standard 2013, Project Professional 2013.

Short Forms Used in This Book and Their Full Meaning.

The following are short forms of keyboard shortcuts used in this Microsoft Office 2013 Keyboard Shortcuts book and their full meaning.

1.	Alt	-	Alternate Key
2.	Caps Lock	-	Caps Lock Key
3.	Ctrl	-	Control Key
4.	Esc	-	Escape Key
5.	F	-	Function Key
6.	Num Lock	-	Number Lock Key
7.	Shft	-	Shift Key
8.	Tab	-	Tabulate Key
9.	Win	-	Windows logo key
10.	Prt sc	-	Print Screen

CHAPTER 1.

Gathering The Basic Knowledge Of Keyboard Shortcuts.

Without the existence of the keyboard, there wouldn't have been anything like keyboard shortcuts, so in this chapter we will learn a little about keyboard before moving to keyboard shortcuts.

1. Definition of Computer Keyboard

This is an input device that is used to send data to the computer memory.

Sketch of a Keyboard

1.1 Types of Keyboard.

   i. Standard (Basic) Keyboard.

   ii. Enhanced (Extended) Keyboard.

   i. **Standard Keyboard:** This is a keyboard designed during the 1800s for mechanical typewriters with just 10 function keys (F keys) placed at the left side of it.

ii. **Enhanced Keyboard:** This is the current 101 to 102-key keyboard that is included in almost all the personal computers (PCs) of nowadays, which has 12 function keys at the top side of it.

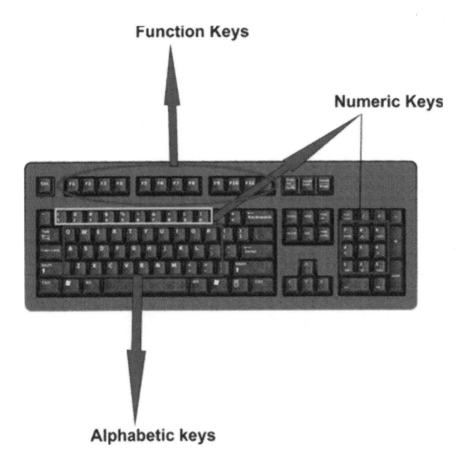

1.2 Segments of the keyboard

- Numeric keys
- Alphabetic keys

- Punctuation Keys
- Windows logo key.
- Function keys
- Special keys

Numeric Keys: Numeric keys are keys with numbers from **0 - 9**.

Alphabetic Keys: These are keys that have alphabets on them, ranging from **A-Z**.

Punctuation Keys: These are keys of the keyboard used for punctuation. Examples include comma, full stop, colon, question marks, hyphen etc.

Windows Logo Key: A key on Microsoft Computer keyboard with its logo displayed on it. Search for this 🪟 on your keyboard.

Function Keys: These are keys that have **F** on them which are usually combined with other keys. They are F1 - F12, and are also in the class called Special Keys.

Special Keys: These are keys that perform special functions. They include: Tab, Ctrl, Caps lock, Insert, Prt sc, alt gr, Shift, Home, Num lock, Esc and many others. Special keys work according to the computer involved. In some keyboard layout, especially laptops, the keys that turn the speaker on/off, the one that increases/decreases the volume, the key that turns the computer Wifi on/off are also special keys.

Other Special Keys Worthy of Note.

Enter Key: This is located at the right-hand corner of the keyboard. It is used to send messages to the computer to execute commands, in most cases it is used to mean "Ok" or "Go".

Escape Key (ESC): This is the first key on the upper left of the keyboard. It is used to cancel routines, close menus and select options such as **Save** according to circumstance.

Control Key (CTRL): It is located on the bottom row of the left and right hand side of the keyboard. They also work with the function keys to execute commands using Keyboard shortcuts (key combinations).

Alternate Key (ALT): It is located on the bottom row also, very close to the CTRL key on both side of the keyboard. It enables many editing functions to be accomplished by using some keystroke combinations on the keyboard.

Shift Key: This adds to the functions of the function keys. In addition, it enables the use of alternative function of a particular button (key), especially, those with more than one function on a key. E.g. use of capital letters, symbols and numbers.

1.3. Selecting/Highlighting With the Keyboard.

This is a highlighting method or style where data is selected using the keyboard instead of a computer mouse.

To do this:

- Move your cursor to the text you want to highlight, make sure that area is active,
- Hold down the shift key with one finger
- Then use another finger to move the arrow key that points to the direction you want to highlight.

1.4 The Operating Modes Of The Keyboard.

Just like the mouse the keyboard has two operating modes. The two modes are Text Entering and Command Mode.

a. **Text Entering Mode:** this mode gives the operator/user the opportunity to type text.

b. **Command Mode:** this is used to command the operating system/software/application to execute commands in certain ways.

2. Ways To Improve In Your Typing Skill.

1. Put Your Eyes Off The Keyboard.

This is the aspect of keyboard usage that many don't find funny because they always ask. "How can I put my eyes off the keyboard when I am running away from the occurrence of errors on my file?" My aim is to be fast, is this not going to slow me down?

Of course, there will be errors and at the same time your speed will slow down but the motive behind the introduction of this method is to make you faster than you are. Looking at your keyboard while you type can make you get a sore neck, it is better you learn to touch type because the more you type with your eyes fixed on the screen instead of the keyboard, the faster you become.

An alternative to keeping your eyes off your keyboard is to use the *"Das Keyboard Ultimate"*.

2. Errors Challenge You

It is better to fail than not to try at all. Not trying at all is an attribute of the weak and lazybones. When you make mistakes, try again because errors are opportunities for improvement.

3. Good Posture (Position Yourself Well).

Do not adopt an awkward position while typing. You should get everything on your desk organized or arranged before sitting to type. Your posture while typing contributes to your speed and productivity.

4. Practice

Here is the conclusion of everything said above. You have to practice your shortcuts constantly. The practice alone is a way of improvement. "Practice brings improvement". Practice always.

2.1 Software That Will Help You Improve In Your Typing Skill.

There are several Software programs for typing that both kids and adults can use for their typing skill. Here is a list of software that can help you improve in your typing: Mavis Beacon, Typing Instructor, Mucky Typing Adventure, Rapid Tying Tutor, Letter Chase Tying Tutor, Alice Touch Typing Tutor and many more. Personally, I recommend Mavis Beacon.

To learn typing with MAVIS BEACON, install Mavis Beacon software to your computer, start with keyboard lesson, then move to games. Games like ***Penguin Crossing, Creature Lab*** or ***Space Junk*** will help you become a professional in typing. Typing and keyboard shortcuts work hand-in-hand.

Sketch of a computer mouse

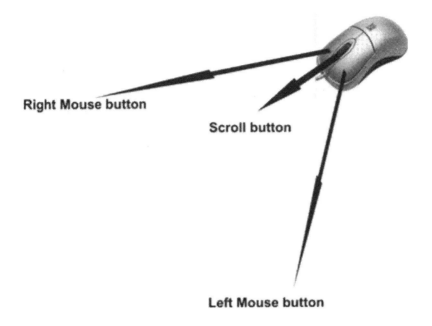

Right Mouse button

Scroll button

Left Mouse button

3. Mouse:

This is an oval shaped portable input device with three buttons for scrolling, left clicking and right clicking that enables work to be done effectively on a computer. The plural form of a mouse is mice.

3.1 Types of Computer Mice

- Mechanical Mouse
- Optical Mechanical Mouse (Optomechanical)
- Laser Mouse
- Optical Mouse
- BlueTrack Mouse

3.2 Forms of Clicking:

Left Clicking: This is the process of clicking the mouse left side button. It can be called *clicking* without the addition of *left*.

Right Clicking: It is the process of clicking the right side button of the mouse.

Double Clicking: It is the process of clicking the left side button two times (twice) and immediately.

Double clicking is used to select a word while thrice clicking is used to select a sentence or paragraph.

Scroll Button: It is the little key attached to the mouse that looks like a tiny wheel. It takes you up and down a page when moved.

3.3 Mouse Pad: This is a small soft mat that is placed under the mouse to make it have a free movement.

3.4 Laptop Mouse Touchpad

This unlike the mouse we explained above is not external, rather it is inbuilt (comes with a laptop computer). With the presence of a laptop mouse touchpad, an external mouse is not needed to use a laptop, except in a case where it is malfunctioning or the operator prefers to use external one for some reasons.

The laptop mouse touchpad is usually positioned at the end of the keyboard section of a laptop computer. It is rectangular in shape with two buttons positioned below it. The two buttons/keys are used for left and right clicking just like the external mouse. Some laptops come with four mouse keys. Two placed above the mouse for left and right clicking and two other keys placed below it for the same function.

4. Definition Of Keyboard Shortcuts.

Keyboard shortcuts are defined as a series of keys, sometimes with combination that execute tasks that typically involve the use of mouse or other input devices.

5. Why You Should Use Keyboard Shortcuts.

1. One may not be able to use a computer mouse easily because of disability or pain.

2. One may not be able to see the mouse pointer as a result of vision impairment, in such case what will the person do? The answer is SHORTCUT.

3. Research has made it known that Extensive mouse usage is related to Repetitive Syndrome Injury (RSI) greatly than the use of keyboard.

4. Keyboard shortcuts speed up computer users, making learning them a worthwhile effort.

5. When performing a job that requires precision, it is wise that you use the keyboard instead of mouse, for instance, if you are dealing with Text Editing, it is better you handle it using keyboard shortcuts than spending more time with mouse alone.

6. Studies calculate that using keyboard shortcuts allows working 10 times faster than working with the mouse. The time you spend looking for the mouse and then getting the cursor to the position you want is lost! Reducing your work duration by 10 times brings you greater results.

5.1 Ways To Become A Lover Of Shortcuts.

1. Always have the urge to learn new shortcut keys associated with the programs you use.
2. Be happy whenever you learn a new shortcut.
3. Try as much as you can to apply the new shortcuts you learnt.
4. Always bear it in mind that learning new shortcuts is worth it.
5. Always remember that use of keyboard shortcuts keeps people healthy while performing computing activities.

5.2 How To Learn New Shortcut Keys

1. Do a research for them: quick reference (a cheat sheet comprehensively arranged) can go a long way to help you improve.
2. Buy applications that show you keyboard shortcuts every time you execute an action with the mouse.
3. Disconnect your mouse if you must learn this fast.
4. Reading user manuals and help topics (Whether offline or online).

5.3 Your Reward For Knowing Shortcut Keys.

1. You will get faster unimaginably.
2. Your level of efficiency will increase.
3. You will find it easy to use.
4. Opportunities are high that you will become an expert in what you do.
5. You won't have to go for **Office button**, click **New,** click **Blank and Recent** and click **Create** just to insert a fresh/blank page. **Ctrl +N** takes care of that in a second.

A Funny Note: Keyboard Shortcuts and Mousing are in a marital union with Keyboard Shortcuts being the head and it will be very bad for anybody to put asunder between them.

5.4 Why We Emphasize On The Use of Shortcuts.
You may never ditch your mouse completely unless you are ready to make your brain a box of keyboard shortcuts which will really be frustrating. Just imagine yourself learning all the shortcuts for the program you use and its various versions. You shouldn't learn keyboard shortcuts like that.

Why we are emphasizing on the use of shortcuts is because mouse usage is becoming unusually common and unhealthy, too. So we just want to make sure both are combined so you can get fast, productive and healthy in your computing activities. All you need to know is just the most useful ones of the programs you use.

CHAPTER 2.

Keyboard Shortcuts In Access 2013.

Definition of Program: Microsoft Access is a well-known electronic database program designed by Microsoft Corporation in 1997 which allows its users to create and manipulate database.

The following list of shortcut keys will help you to excel in Microsoft Access.

Access Web App Shortcut Keys

Design-time shortcut keys

These shortcut keys are available when you are customizing a web app in Access. Some of the shortcuts listed under Desktop database shortcut keys are also available when customizing a web app.

TASK	SHORTCUT
Advance through all tables and views (when not in Edit mode)	TAB
Move a table or view selector	Arrow keys
Show or hide the Navigation Pane	F11
Advance through the controls on a view (when in Edit mode)	TAB
Move the selected control(s)	Arrow keys
Open or close the properties for the selected control	F4
Show or hide the Field List	Alt+F8

Runtime (browser) shortcut keys

These shortcut keys are available when you are using an Access web app in the browser. You can also use any shortcut keys that are provided by the browser itself.

TASK	SHORTCUT
New item	N
Delete item	Delete
Edit item	E
Save item	Ctrl+S
Cancel	Escape
Edit filter	/
Close a popup view	Escape

When working in the browser, press Tab, Shift+Tab, and the arrow keys to move between the table list, the view selector, the action bar, the search box, and controls on views.

Desktop Database Shortcut Keys For Access.

Global Access Shortcut Keys

Opening databases

TASK	SHORTCUT
Open a new database	CTRL+N
Open an existing database	CTRL+O

Printing and Saving

TASK	SHORTCUT
Print the current or selected object	CTRL+P

Open the **Print** dialog box from **Print Preview**	P or CTRL+P
Open the **Page Setup** dialog box from **Print Preview**	S
Cancel Print Preview or Layout Preview	C or ESC
Save a database object	CTRL+S or SHIFT+F12
Open the **Save As** dialog box	F12

Using a combo box or list box

TASK	SHORTCUT
Open a combo box	F4 or ALT+DOWN ARROW
Refresh the contents of a Lookup field list box or combo box	F9
Move down one line	DOWN ARROW
Move down one page	PAGE DOWN
Move up one line	UP ARROW
Move up one page	PAGE UP
Exit the combo box or list box	TAB

Finding and replacing text or data

TASK	SHORTCUT
Open the **Find** tab in the **Find and Replace** dialog box (Datasheet view and Form view only)	CTRL+F
Open the **Replace** tab in the **Find and Replace** dialog box (Datasheet view and Form view only)	CTRL+H
Find the next occurrence of the text specified in the **Find and Replace**	SHIFT+F4

dialog box when the dialog box is closed (Datasheet view and Form view only)	

Working in Design, Layout, or Datasheet View

TASK	SHORTCUT
Switch between Edit mode (with insertion point displayed) and Navigation mode in a datasheet. When working in a form or report, press ESC to leave Navigation mode.	F2
Switch to the property sheet (Design view and Layout view in forms and reports)	F4
Switch to Form view from form Design view	F5
Switch between the upper and lower portions of a window (Design view of queries, and the Advanced Filter/Sort window)	F6
Cycle through the field grid, field properties, the Navigation Pane, access keys in the Keyboard Access System, Zoom controls, and the security bar (Design view of tables)	F6
Open the **Choose Builder** dialog box from a selected control on a form or report (Design view only)	F7
Open the Visual Basic Editor from a selected property in the property sheet for a form or report	F7
Switch from the Visual Basic Editor back to form or report Design view	ALT+F11

Editing Controls in Form and Report Design View

TASK	SHORTCUT
Copy the selected control to the Clipboard	CTRL+C
Cut the selected control and copy it to the Clipboard	CTRL+X
Paste the contents of the Clipboard in the upper-left corner of the selected section	CTRL+V
Move the selected control to the right (except controls that are part of a layout)	RIGHT ARROW or CTRL+RIGHT ARROW
Move the selected control to the left (except controls that are part of a layout)	LEFT ARROW or CTRL+LEFT ARROW
Move the selected control up (except controls that are part of a layout)	UP ARROW or CTRL+UP ARROW
Move the selected control down (except controls that are part of a layout)	DOWN ARROW or CTRL+DOWN ARROW
Increase the height of the selected control **Note:** If used with controls that are in a layout, the entire row of the layout is resized.	SHIFT+DOWN ARROW
Increase the width of the selected control **Note:** If used with controls that are in a layout, the entire column of the layout is resized.	SHIFT+RIGHT ARROW

Reduce the height of the selected control **Note:** If used with controls that are in a layout, the entire row of the layout is resized.	SHIFT+UP ARROW
Reduce the width of the selected control **Note:** If used with controls that are in a layout, the entire column of the layout is resized.	SHIFT+LEFT ARROW

Window Operations

By default, Access databases display as tabbed documents. To use windowed documents, Click the **File** tab., and then click **Options**. In the **Access Options** dialog box, click **Current Database** and, under **Document Window Options**, click **Overlapping Windows**.

Note: You will have to close and reopen the current database for the option to take effect.

TASK	SHORTCUT
Toggle the Navigation Pane	F11
Cycle between open windows	CTRL+F6
Restore the selected minimized window when all windows are minimized	ENTER
Turn on Resize mode for the active window when it is not maximized; press the arrow keys to resize the window, then press Enter to apply the new size.	CTRL+F8

Display the control menu	ALT+SPACEBAR
Display the shortcut menu	Shortcut menu key (near the lower right of most keyboards)
Close the active window	CTRL+W or CTRL+F4
Switch between the Visual Basic Editor and the previous active window	ALT+F11

Working With Wizards

TASK	SHORTCUT
Toggle the focus forward between controls in the wizard	TAB
Move to the next page of the wizard	ALT+N
Move to the previous page of the wizard	ALT+B
Complete the wizard	ALT+F

Miscellaneous

TASK	SHORTCUT
Display the complete hyperlink address for a selected hyperlink	F2
Check spelling	F7
Open the Zoom box to conveniently enter expressions and other text in small input areas	SHIFT+F2
Display a property sheet in Design view	ALT+ENTER
Exit Access	ALT+F4
Invoke a Builder	CTRL+F2

Toggle forward between views when in a table, query, form, or report. If there are additional views available, successive keystrokes will move to the next available view.	CTRL+RIGHT ARROW or CRTL+COMMA (,)
Toggle back between views when in a table, query, form, or report. If there are additional views available, successive keystrokes will move to the previous view. **Note:** CTRL+PERIOD (.) does not work under all conditions with all objects.	CTRL+LEFT ARROW or CRTL+PERIOD (.)

The Navigation Pane Shortcut Keys

TASK	SHORTCUT
Show or hide the Navigation Pane	F11
Go to the Navigation Pane Search box (if focus is already on the Navigation Pane)	CTRL+F

Editing and Navigating the Object List

TASK	SHORTCUT
Rename a selected object	F2
Move down one line	DOWN ARROW
Move down one window	PAGE DOWN
Move to the last object	END
Move up one line	UP ARROW
Move up one window	PAGE UP

Navigating and Opening Objects

TASK	SHORTCUT
Open the selected table or query in Datasheet view	ENTER
Open the selected form or report	ENTER
Run the selected macro	ENTER
Open the selected table, query, form, report, macro, or module in Design view	CTRL+ENTER
Display the Immediate window in the Visual Basic Editor	CTRL+G

Work with Menus

TASK	SHORTCUT
Show the shortcut menu	Shortcut key (near the lower right of most keyboards)
Show the access keys	ALT or F10
Show the program icon menu (on the program title bar)	ALT+SPACEBAR
With the menu or submenu visible, select the next or previous command	DOWN ARROW or UP ARROW
Select the menu to the left or right; or, when a submenu is visible, to switch between the main menu and the submenu	LEFT ARROW or RIGHT ARROW
Select the first or last command on the menu or submenu	HOME or END
Close the visible menu and submenu at the same time	ALT

Close the visible menu; or, with a submenu visible, to close the submenu only	ESC

Work in Windows and Dialog Boxes

Using a Program Window

TASK	SHORTCUT
Switch to the next program	ALT+TAB
Switch to the previous program	ALT+SHIFT+TAB
Show the Windows **Start** menu	CTRL+ESC
Close the active database window	CTRL+W
Switch to the next database window	CTRL+F6
Switch to the previous database window	CTRL+SHIFT+F6
Restore the selected minimized window when all windows are minimized	ENTER

Using a dialog box

TASK	SHORTCUT
Switch to the next tab in a dialog box	CTRL+TAB
Switch to the previous tab in a dialog box	CTRL+SHIFT+TAB
Move to the next option or option group	TAB
Move to the previous option or option group	SHIFT+TAB
Move between options in the selected drop-down list box, or to move between some	Arrow keys

options in a group of options	
Perform the action assigned to the selected button; select or clear the check box	SPACEBAR
Move to the option by the first letter in the option name in a drop-down list box	Letter key for the first letter in the option name you want (when a drop-down list box is selected)
Select the option, or to select or clear the check box by the letter underlined in the option name	ALT+letter key
Open the selected drop-down list box	ALT+DOWN ARROW
Close the selected drop-down list box	ESC
Perform the action assigned to the default button in the dialog box	ENTER
Cancel the command and close the dialog box	ESC

Editing in a text box

TASK	SHORTCUT
Move to the beginning of the entry	HOME
Move to the end of the entry	END
Move one character to the left or right	LEFT ARROW or RIGHT ARROW

Move one word to the left or right	CTRL+LEFT ARROW or CTRL+RIGHT ARROW
Select from the insertion point to the beginning of the text entry	SHIFT+HOME
Select from the insertion point to the end of the text entry	SHIFT+END
Change the selection by one character to the left	SHIFT+LEFT ARROW
Change the selection by one character to the right	SHIFT+RIGHT ARROW
Change the selection by one word to the left	CTRL+SHIFT+LEFT ARROW
Change the selection by one word to the right	CTRL+SHIFT+RIGHT ARROW

Work with property sheets

Using a property sheet with a form or report in Design view or Layout view

TASK	SHORTCUT
Show or hide the Property Sheet	F4
Move among choices in the control selection drop-down list one item at a time	DOWN ARROW or UP ARROW
Move among choices in the control selection drop-down list one page at a time	PAGE DOWN or PAGE UP
Move to the property sheet tabs from the control selection drop-down list	TAB

Move among the property sheet tabs with a tab selected, but no property selected	LEFT ARROW or RIGHT ARROW
With a property already selected, move down one property on a tab	TAB
With a property selected, move up one property on a tab; or if already at the top, move to the tab	SHIFT+TAB
Toggle forward between tabs when a property is selected	CTRL+TAB
Toggle backward between tabs when a property is selected	CTRL+SHIFT+TAB

Using a property sheet with a table or query in Design view

TASK	SHORTCUT
Show or hide the Property Sheet	F4
With a tab selected, but no property selected, move among the property sheet tabs	LEFT ARROW or RIGHT ARROW
Move to the property sheet tabs when a property is selected	CTRL+TAB
Move to the first property of a tab when no property is selected	TAB
Move down one property on a tab	TAB
Move up one property on a tab; or if already at the top, select the tab itself	SHIFT+TAB

Toggle forward between tabs when a property is selected	CTRL+TAB
Toggle backward between tabs when a property is selected	CTRL+SHIFT+TAB

Using the Field List pane with a form or report in Design view or Layout view

TASK	SHORTCUT
Show or hide the **Field List** pane	ALT+F8
Add the selected field to the form or report detail section	ENTER
Move up or down the **Field List** pane	UP ARROW or DOWN ARROW
Move between the upper and lower panes of the **Field List**	TAB

Shortcut Keys For Working With Text And Data In Access

Select text and data

Selecting text in a field

TASK	SHORTCUT
Change the size of the selection by one character to the right	SHIFT+RIGHT ARROW
Change the size of the selection by one word to the right	CTRL+SHIFT+RIGHT ARROW
Change the size of the selection by one character to the left	SHIFT+LEFT ARROW

Change the size of the selection by one word to the left	CTRL+SHIFT+LEFT ARROW

Selecting a field or record

Note: To cancel a selection, use the opposite arrow key.

TASK	SHORTCUT
Select the next field	TAB
Switch between Edit mode (with insertion point displayed) and Navigation mode in a datasheet. When using a form or report, press ESC to leave Navigation mode.	F2
Switch between selecting the current record and the first field of the current record, in Navigation mode	SHIFT+SPACEBAR
Extend selection to the previous record, if the current record is selected	SHIFT+UP ARROW
Extend selection to the next record, if the current record is selected	SHIFT+DOWN ARROW
Select all records	CTRL+A or CTRL+SHIFT+SPACEBAR

Extending a selection

TASK	SHORTCUT
Turn on Extend mode (in Datasheet view, **Extended Selection** appears	F8

in the lower-right corner of the window); pressing F8 repeatedly extends the selection to the word, the field, the record, and all records	
Extend a selection to adjacent fields in the same row in Datasheet view	LEFT ARROW or RIGHT ARROW
Extend a selection to adjacent rows in Datasheet view	UP ARROW or DOWN ARROW
Undo the previous extension	SHIFT+F8
Cancel Extend mode	ESC

Selecting and moving a column in Datasheet view

TASK	SHORTCUT
Select the current column or cancel the column selection, in Navigation mode only	CTRL+SPACEBAR
Extend the selection one column to the right, if the current column is selected	SHIFT+RIGHT ARROW
Extend the selection one column to the left, if the current column is selected	SHIFT+LEFT ARROW
Turn on Move mode; then press the RIGHT ARROW or LEFT ARROW key to move selected column(s) to the right or left	CTRL+SHIFT+F8

Edit text and data

Note: If the insertion point is not visible, press F2 to display it.

Moving the insertion point in a field

TASK	SHORTCUT
Move the insertion point one character to the right	RIGHT ARROW
Move the insertion point one word to the right	CTRL+RIGHT ARROW
Move the insertion point one character to the left	LEFT ARROW
Move the insertion point one word to the left	CTRL+LEFT ARROW
Move the insertion point to the end of the field, in single-line fields; or to move it to the end of the line in multi-line fields	END
Move the insertion point to the end of the field, in multiple-line fields	CTRL+END
Move the insertion point to the beginning of the field, in single-line fields; or to move it to the beginning of the line in multi-line fields	HOME
Move the insertion point to the beginning of the field, in multiple-line fields	CTRL+HOME

Copying, moving, or deleting text

TASK	SHORTCUT
Copy the selection to the Clipboard	CTRL+C
Cut the selection and copy it to the Clipboard	CTRL+X
Paste the contents of the Clipboard at the insertion point	CTRL+V
Delete the selection or the character to the left of the insertion point	BACKSPACE
Delete the selection or the character to the right of the insertion point	DELETE

Delete all characters to the right of the insertion point	CTRL+DELETE

Undoing changes

TASK	SHORTCUT
Undo typing	CTRL+Z or ALT+BACKSPACE
Undo changes in the current field or current record; if both have been changed, press ESC twice to undo changes, first in the current field and then in the current record	ESC

Entering data in Datasheet or Form view

TASK	SHORTCUT
Insert the current date	CTRL+SEMICOLON (;)
Insert the current time	CTRL+SHIFT+COLON (:)
Insert the default value for a field	CTRL+ALT+SPACEBAR
Insert the value from the same field in the previous record	CTRL+APOSTROPHE (')
Add a new record	CTRL+PLUS SIGN (+)
In a datasheet, delete the current record	CTRL+MINUS SIGN (-)
Save changes to the current record	SHIFT+ENTER
Switch between the values in a check box or option button	SPACEBAR
Insert a new line in a Short Text or Long Text field	CTRL+ENTER

Refreshing fields with current data

TASK	SHORTCUT
Recalculate the fields in the window	F9
Requery the underlying tables; in a subform, this requires the underlying table for the subform only	SHIFT+F9
Refresh the contents of a Lookup field list box or combo box	F9

Shortcut keys for navigating records in Access

Navigate in Design view

TASK	SHORTCUT
Switch between Edit mode (with insertion point displayed) and Navigation mode	F2
Toggle the property sheet	F4 or ALT+ENTER
Switch to Form view from form Design view	F5
Switch between the upper and lower portions of a window (Design view of macros, queries, and the Advanced Filter/Sort window) Use F6 when the TAB key does not take you to the section of the screen you want.	F6
Toggle forward between the design pane, properties, Navigation Pane, access keys, and Zoom controls (Design view of tables, forms, and reports)	F6

Open the Visual Basic Editor from a selected property in the property sheet for a form or report	F7
Invokes the **Field List** pane in a form, or report. If the **Field List** pane is already open, focus moves to the **Field List** pane.	ALT+F8
When you have a code module open, switch from the Visual Basic Editor to form or report Design view	SHIFT+F7
Switch from a control's property sheet in form or report Design view to the design surface without changing the control focus	SHIFT+F7
Copy the selected control to the Clipboard	CTRL+C
Cut the selected control and copy it to the Clipboard	CTRL+X
Paste the contents of the Clipboard in the upper-left corner of the selected section	CTRL+V
Move the selected control to the right by a pixel along the page's grid	RIGHT ARROW
Move the selected control to the left by a pixel along the page's grid	LEFT ARROW
Move the selected control up by a pixel along the page's grid **Note:** For controls in a stacked layout, this switches the position of the selected control with the control directly above it, unless it is already the uppermost control in the layout.	UP ARROW

Move the selected control down by a pixel along the page's grid **Note:** For controls in a stacked layout, this switches the position of the selected control with the control directly below it, unless it is already the lowermost control in the layout.	DOWN ARROW
Move the selected control to the right by a pixel (irrespective of the page's grid)	CTRL+RIGHT ARROW
Move the selected control to the left by a pixel (irrespective of the page's grid)	CTRL+LEFT ARROW
Move the selected control up by a pixel (irrespective of the page's grid) **Note:** For controls in a stacked layout, this switches the position of the selected control with the control directly above it, unless it is already the uppermost control in the layout.	CTRL+UP ARROW
Move the selected control down by a pixel (irrespective of the page's grid) **Note:** For controls in a stacked layout, this switches the position of the selected control with the control directly below it, unless it is already the lowermost control in the layout.	CTRL+DOWN ARROW
Increase the width of the selected control (to the right) by a pixel **Note:** For controls in a stacked layout, this increases the width of the whole layout.	SHIFT+RIGHT ARROW

Decrease the width of the selected control (to the left) by a pixel **Note:** For controls in a stacked layout, this decreases the width of the whole layout.	SHIFT+LEFT ARROW
Decrease the height of the selected control (from the bottom) by a pixel	SHIFT+UP ARROW
Increase the height of the selected control (from the bottom) by a pixel	SHIFT+DOWN ARROW

Navigate in Datasheet view

Going to a specific record

TASK	SHORTCUT
Move to the record number box; then type the record number and press ENTER	F5

Navigating between fields and records

TASK	SHORTCUT
Move to the next field	TAB or RIGHT ARROW
Move to the last field in the current record, in Navigation mode	END
Move to the previous field	SHIFT+TAB, or LEFT ARROW
Move to the first field in the current record, in Navigation mode	HOME
Move to the current field in the next record	DOWN ARROW

Move to the current field in the last record, in Navigation mode	CTRL+DOWN ARROW
Move to the last field in the last record, in Navigation mode	CTRL+END
Move to the current field in the previous record	UP ARROW
Move to the current field in the first record, in Navigation mode	CTRL+UP ARROW
Move to the first field in the first record, in Navigation mode	CTRL+HOME

Navigating to another screen of data

TASK	SHORTCUT
Move down one screen	PAGE DOWN
Move up one screen	PAGE UP
Move right one screen	CTRL+PAGE DOWN
Move left one screen	CTRL+PAGE UP

Navigate in subdatasheets

Going to a specific record

TASK	SHORTCUT
Move from the subdatasheet to move to the record number box; then type the record number and press ENTER	ALT+F5

Expanding and collapsing subdatasheet

TASK	SHORTCUT
Move from the datasheet to expand the record's subdatasheet	CTRL+SHIFT+DOWN ARROW
Collapse the subdatasheet	CTRL+SHIFT+UP ARROW

Navigating between the datasheet and subdatasheet

TASK	SHORTCUT
Enter the subdatasheet from the last field of the previous record in the datasheet	TAB
Enter the subdatasheet from the first field of the following record in the datasheet	SHIFT+TAB
Exit the subdatasheet and move to the first field of the next record in the datasheet	CTRL+TAB
Exit the subdatasheet and move to the last field of the previous record in the datasheet	CTRL+SHIFT+TAB
From the last field in the subdatasheet to enter the next field in the datasheet	TAB
From the datasheet to bypass the subdatasheet and move to the next record in the datasheet	DOWN ARROW
From the datasheet to bypass the subdatasheet and move to the previous record in the datasheet	UP ARROW

Note: You can navigate between fields and records in a subdatasheet with the same shortcut keys used in Datasheet view.

Navigate in Form view

Going to a specific record

TASK	SHORTCUT
Move to the record number box; then type the record number and press ENTER	F5

Navigating between fields and records

TASK	SHORTCUT
Move to the next field	TAB
Move to the previous field	SHIFT+TAB
Move to the last control on the form and remain in the current record, in Navigation mode	END
Move to the last control on the form and set focus in the last record, in Navigation mode	CTRL+END
Move to the first control on the form and remain in the current record, in Navigation mode	HOME
Move to the first control on the form and set focus in the first record, in Navigation mode	CTRL+HOME
Move to the current field in the next record	CTRL+PAGE DOWN
Move to the current field in the previous record	CTRL+PAGE UP

Navigating in forms with more than one page

TASK	SHORTCUT
Move down one page; at the end of the record, moves to the equivalent page on the next record	PAGE DOWN

Move up one page; at the end of the record, moves to the equivalent page on the previous record	PAGE UP

Navigating between a main form and a subform

TASK	SHORTCUT
Enter the subform from the preceding field in the main form	TAB
Enter the subform from the following field in the main form	SHIFT+TAB
Exit the subform and move to the next field in the master form or next record	CTRL+TAB
Exit the subform and move to the previous field in the main form or previous record	CTRL+SHIFT+TAB

Navigate in Print Preview and Layout Preview

Dialog box and window operations

TASK	SHORTCUT
Open the **Print** dialog box from Print	CTRL+P (for datasheets, forms, and reports)
Open the **Page Setup** dialog box (forms and reports only)	S
Zoom in or out on a part of the page	Z
Cancel Print Preview or Layout Preview	C or ESC

Viewing Different Pages

TASK	SHORTCUT
Move to the page number box; then type the page number and press ENTER	ALT+F5
View the next page (when **Fit To Window** is selected)	PAGE DOWN or DOWN ARROW
View the previous page (when **Fit To Window** is selected)	PAGE UP or UP ARROW

Navigating in Print Preview and Layout Preview

TASK	SHORTCUT
Scroll down in small increments	DOWN ARROW
Scroll down one full screen	PAGE DOWN
Move to the bottom of the page	CTRL+DOWN ARROW
Scroll up in small increments	UP ARROW
Scroll up one full screen	PAGE UP
Move to the top of the page	CTRL+UP ARROW
Scroll to the right in small increments	RIGHT ARROW
Move to the right edge of the page	END
Move to the lower-right corner of the page	CTRL+END
Scroll to the left in small increments	LEFT ARROW
Move to the left edge of the page	HOME
Move to the upper-left corner of the page	CTRL+HOME

Any Pane

TASK	SHORTCUT
Move among the Query Designer panes	F6, SHIFT+F6

Diagram Pane

TASK	SHORTCUT
Move among tables, views, and functions, (and to join lines, if available)	TAB, or SHIFT+TAB
Move between columns in a table, view, or function	Arrow keys
Choose the selected data column for output	SPACEBAR or PLUS key
Remove the selected data column from the query output	SPACEBAR or MINUS key
Remove the selected table, view, or function, or join line from the query	DELETE

Note: If multiple items are selected, pressing SPACEBAR affects all selected items. Select multiple items by holding down the SHIFT key while clicking them. Toggle the selected state of a single item by holding down CTRL while clicking it.

Grid Pane

TASK	SHORTCUT
Move among cells	Arrow keys or TAB or SHIFT+TAB
Move to the last row in the current column	CTRL+DOWN ARROW
Move to the first row in the current column	CTRL+UP ARROW

Move to the top left cell in the visible portion of grid	CTRL+HOME
Move to the bottom right cell	CTRL+END
Move in a drop-down list	UP ARROW or DOWN ARROW
Select an entire grid column	CTRL+SPACEBAR
Toggle between edit mode and cell selection mode	F2
Copy selected text in cell to the Clipboard (in edit mode)	CTRL+C
Cut selected text in cell and place it on the Clipboard (in edit mode)	CTRL+X
Paste text from the Clipboard (in edit mode)	CTRL+V
Toggle between insert and overstrike mode while editing in a cell	INS
Toggle the check box in the Output column **Note:** If multiple items are selected, pressing this key affects all selected items.	SPACEBAR
Clear the selected contents of a cell	DELETE
Clear all values for a selected grid column	DELETE

SQL Pane

You can use the standard Windows editing keys when working in the SQL pane, such as CTRL+ arrow keys to move between words, and the **Cut**, **Copy**, and **Paste** commands on the **Home** tab.

Note: You can only insert text; there is no overstrike mode.

Shortcut Keys For Access Ribbon Commands

Ribbon Keyboard Shortcuts

1. Press ALT.

   The KeyTips are displayed over each feature that is available in the current view.

2. Press the letter shown in the KeyTip over the feature that you want to use.
3. Depending on which letter you press, you might be shown additional KeyTips. For example, if the **External Data** tab is active and you press C, the **Create** tab is displayed, along with the KeyTips for the groups on that tab.
4. Continue pressing letters until you press the letter of the command or control that you want to use. In some cases, you must first press the letter of the group that contains the command.

Note: To cancel the action that you are taking and hide the KeyTips, press ALT.

Online Help

Keyboard Shortcuts for Using the Help Window

The Help window provides access to all Office Help content. The Help window displays topics and other Help content.

In the Help window

TASK	SHORTCUT
Open the Help window.	F1
Switch between the Help window and the active program.	ALT+TAB
Go back to **Program Name** Home.	ALT+HOME
Select the next item in the Help window.	TAB
Select the previous item in the Help window.	SHIFT+TAB
Perform the action for the selected item.	ENTER
In the **Browse Program Name Help** section of the Help window, select the next or previous item, respectively.	TAB or SHIFT+TAB
In the **Browse Program Name Help** section of the Help window, expand or collapse the selected item, respectively.	ENTER
Select the next hidden text or hyperlink, including **Show All** or **Hide All** at the top of a topic.	TAB
Select the previous hidden text or hyperlink.	SHIFT+TAB
Perform the action for the selected **Show All**, **Hide All**, hidden text, or hyperlink.	ENTER
Move back to the previous Help topic (**Back** button).	ALT+LEFT ARROW or BACKSPACE
Move forward to the next Help topic (**Forward** button).	ALT+RIGHT ARROW

Scroll small amounts up or down, respectively, within the currently displayed Help topic.	UP ARROW, DOWN ARROW
Scroll larger amounts up or down, respectively, within the currently displayed Help topic.	PAGE UP, PAGE DOWN
Stop the last action (**Stop** button).	ESC
Refresh the window (**Refresh** button).	F5
Print the current Help topic. **Note:** If the cursor is not in the current Help topic, press F6, and then press CTRL+P.	CTRL+P
Change the connection state.	F6, and then press ENTER to open the list of choices
Switch among areas in the Help window; for example, switch between the toolbar and the **Search** list.	F6
In a Table of Contents in tree view, select the next or previous item, respectively.	UP ARROW, DOWN ARROW
In a Table of Contents in tree view, expand or collapse the selected item, respectively.	LEFT ARROW, RIGHT ARROW

Microsoft Office Basics

Use Open and Save As in the Backstage

TASK	SHORTCUT
View **Open** in the Backstage.	Ctrl+O
View **Save As** in the Backstage.	Ctrl+S

Continue saving an Office file (after giving the file a name and location)	Ctrl+S
View **Save As** in the Backstage (after giving the file a name and location)	Alt+F+S
Return to your Office file.	Esc

Use the Open and Save As Dialog Boxes

TASK	SHORTCUT
View the **Open** dialog box.	Ctrl+F12
View the **Save As** dialog box.	F12
Open the selected folder or file.	ENTER
Open the folder one level above the selected folder.	BACKSPACE
Delete the selected folder or file.	DELETE
Display a shortcut menu for a selected item such as a folder or file.	SHIFT+F10
Move forward through options.	TAB
Move back through options.	SHIFT+TAB
Open the **Look in** list.	F4 or ALT+I

Display and Use Windows

TASK	SHORTCUT
Switch to the next window.	ALT+TAB
Switch to the previous window.	ALT+SHIFT+TAB
Close the active window.	CTRL+W or CTRL+F4
Move to a task pane from another pane in the program window (clockwise direction). You might need to press F6 more than once. **Note:** If pressing F6 doesn't display the task pane you want, try	F6

pressing ALT to place focus on the ribbon and then pressing CTRL+TAB to move to the task pane.	
When more than one window is open, switch to the next window.	CTRL+F6
Switch to the previous window.	CTRL+SHIFT+F6
When a document window is not maximized, perform the **Size** command (on the **Control** menu for the window). Press the arrow keys to resize the window, and, when finished, press ENTER.	CTRL+F8
Minimize a window to an icon (works for only some Microsoft Office programs).	CTRL+F9
Maximize or restore a selected window.	CTRL+F10
Copy a picture of the screen to the Clipboard.	PRINT SCREEN
Copy a picture of the selected window to the Clipboard.	ALT+PRINT SCREEN

Move Around in Text or Cells

TASK	SHORTCUT
Move one character to the left.	LEFT ARROW
Move one character to the right.	RIGHT ARROW
Move one line up.	UP ARROW
Move one line down.	DOWN ARROW
Move one word to the left.	CTRL+LEFT ARROW
Move one word to the right.	CTRL+RIGHT ARROW
Move to the end of a line.	END
Move to the beginning of a line.	HOME

Move up one paragraph.	CTRL+UP ARROW
Move down one paragraph.	CTRL+DOWN ARROW
Move to the end of a text box.	CTRL+END
Move to the beginning of a text box.	CTRL+HOME
Repeat the last **Find** action.	SHIFT+F4

Move Around in and Work in Tables

TASK	SHORTCUT
Move to the next cell.	TAB
Move to the preceding cell.	SHIFT+TAB
Move to the next row.	DOWN ARROW
Move to the preceding row.	UP ARROW
Insert a tab in a cell.	CTRL+TAB
Start a new paragraph.	ENTER
Add a new row at the bottom of the table.	TAB at the end of the last row

Access and Use Task Panes

TASK	SHORTCUT
Move to a task pane from another pane in the program window. (You might need to press F6 more than once.) **Note:** If pressing F6 doesn't display the task pane you want, try pressing ALT to place the focus on the ribbon and then pressing CTRL+TAB to move to the task pane.	F6

When a task pane is active, select the next or previous option in the task pane.	TAB or SHIFT+TAB
Display the full set of commands on the task pane menu.	CTRL+DOWN ARROW
Move among choices on a selected submenu; move among certain options in a group of options in a dialog box.	DOWN ARROW or UP ARROW
Open the selected menu, or perform the action assigned to the selected button.	SPACEBAR or ENTER
Open a shortcut menu; open a drop-down menu for the selected gallery item.	SHIFT+F10
When a menu or submenu is visible, select the first or last command on the menu or submenu.	HOME or END
Scroll up or down in the selected gallery list.	PAGE UP or PAGE DOWN
Move to the top or bottom of the selected gallery list.	CTRL+HOME or CTRL+END

Tips

Use Dialog Boxes

TASK	SHORTCUT
Move to the next option or option group.	TAB
Move to the previous option or option group.	SHIFT+TAB
Switch to the next tab in a dialog box.	CTRL+TAB

Switch to the previous tab in a dialog box.	CTRL+SHIFT+TAB
Move between options in an open drop-down list, or between options in a group of options.	Arrow keys
Perform the action assigned to the selected button; select or clear the selected check box.	SPACEBAR
Open the list if it is closed and move to that option in the list.	First letter of an option in a drop-down list
Select an option; select or clear a check box.	ALT+ the letter underlined in an option
Open a selected drop-down list.	ALT+DOWN ARROW
Close a selected drop-down list; cancel a command and close a dialog box.	ESC
Perform the action assigned to a default button in a dialog box.	ENTER

Use Edit Boxes Within Dialog Boxes

An edit box is a blank in which you type or paste an entry, such as your user name or the path of a folder.

TASK	SHORTCUT
Move to the beginning of the entry.	HOME
Move to the end of the entry.	END

Move one character to the left or right.	LEFT ARROW or RIGHT ARROW
Move one word to the left.	CTRL+LEFT ARROW
Move one word to the right.	CTRL+RIGHT ARROW
Select or cancel selection one character to the left.	SHIFT+LEFT ARROW
Select or cancel selection one character to the right.	SHIFT+RIGHT ARROW
Select or cancel selection one word to the left.	CTRL+SHIFT+LEFT ARROW
Select or cancel selection one word to the right.	CTRL+SHIFT+RIGHT ARROW
Select from the insertion point to the beginning of the entry.	SHIFT+HOME
Select from the insertion point to the end of the entry.	SHIFT+END

CHAPTER 3.

Keyboard Shortcuts In Publisher 2013.

Definition of Program: Microsoft Publisher is a program designed by Microsoft in 1991 for Desktop Publishing. It is included in Office 2013 bundle.

The following list of shortcut keys will help you to excel in Microsoft Publisher.

Ribbon Shortcuts.

These shortcuts were introduced with the Publisher ribbon. Some tabs are contextual and appear only when you've inserted or selected an object such as a shape or a table. The double-letter shortcuts make it possible to use keyboard shortcuts with contextual tabs.

To use these, first selected the object, then press Alt, press the two letter context menu shortcut, and then press the remaining keys if any. For example to open the **Shape Effects** menu and add a shadow to a shape you select the shape, press **Alt, JD** to open the **Drawing Tools – Format** tab, **SE** to open the **Shape Effects** menu, **S** to select the **Shadow Gallery**, and then tab through the shadow options to apply the shadow to your shape.

Shape and Picture Effects

Shape Effects

TASK	SHORTCUT

Open the **Shape Effects Menu**	Alt, JD, SE
Open the **Shape Effects – Shadow Gallery**	Alt, JD, SE, S - then tab through options
Open the **Shape Effects – Reflection Gallery**	Alt, JD, SE, R - then tab through options
Open the **Shape Effects – Glow Gallery**	Alt, JD,SE,G- then tab through options
Open the **Shape Effects – Soft Edges Gallery**	Alt, JD,SE,E - then tab through options
Open the **Shape Effects – Bevel Gallery**	Alt, JD,SE,B - then tab through options
Open the **Shape Effects – 3-D Rotation Gallery**	Alt, JD,SE,D - then tab through options
Open the **Shape Styles Gallery**	Alt, JD,ST - then tab through options

Picture effects

TASK	SHORTCUT
Open the **Picture Effects Menu**	Alt, JP,PE
Open the **Picture Effects – Shadow Gallery**	Alt, JP,PE,S - then tab through options
Open the **Picture Effects – Reflection Gallery**	Alt, JP,PE,R - then tab through options
Open the **Picture Effects – Glow Gallery**	Alt, JP,PE,G - then tab through options
Open the **Picture Effects – Soft Edges Gallery**	Alt, JP,PE,E - then tab through options
Open the **Picture Effects – Bevel Gallery**	Alt, JP,PE,B - then tab through options
Open the **Picture Effects – 3-D Rotation Gallery**	Alt, JP,PE,D - then tab through options
Open the **Picture Styles Gallery**	Alt, JP,K - then tab through options
Clear **Picture Style**	Alt, JP,K,C

Text Effects

Text fill dropdown

TASK	SHORTCUT
Open Text Fill Dropdown	Alt, JX,TI
No Fill	Alt, JX,TI,N - then tab through options
More Fill Colors...	Alt, JX,TI,M - then tab through options
Fill Effects...	Alt, JX,TI,F - then tab through options
Tints	Alt, JX,TI,T - then tab through options
Sample Font Color	Alt, JX,TI,S

Text outline dropdown

TASK	SHORTCUT
Open Text Outline Dropdown	Alt ,JX,TO
No Outline	Alt ,JX,TO,N
More Outline Colors...	Alt, JX,TO,M - then tab through options
Outline Effects...	Alt. JX.TO.O - then tab through options
Sample Line Color	Alt, JX,TO,S - then tab through options
Weight	Alt, JX,TO,W - then tab through options
Dashes	Alt, JX,TO,D - then tab through options

Text effects dropdown

TASK	SHORTCUT
Open Text Effects Dropdown	Alt, JX,TE

Shadow	Alt, JX, TE,S - then tab through options
Reflection	Alt, JX, TE,R - then tab through options
Glow	Alt, JX, TE,G - then tab through options
Bevel	Alt, JX, TE,B - then tab through options

Create, Open, Close, Or Save A Publication

Create, open, close a publication

TASK	SHORTCUT
Open a new instance of Publisher	CTRL+N
Display the **Open Publication** dialog box	CTRL+O
Close the current publication	CTRL+F4 or CTRL+W
Display the **Save As** dialog box	CTRL+S

Edit Or Format Text Or Objects

Edit or format text

TASK	SHORTCUT
Display the **Find and Replace** task pane, with the **Find** option selected	F3 or CTRL+F or SHIFT+F4
Display the **Find and Replace** task pane, with the **Replace** option selected	CTRL+H
Check spelling	F7
Display the **Thesaurus** task pane	SHIFT+F7

Display the **Research** task pane	ALT + click a word
Select all the text (If the cursor is in a text box, this selects all text in the current story; if the cursor is not in a text box, this selects all the objects on a page.)	CTRL+A
Make text bold	CTRL+B
Italicize text	CTRL+I
Underline text	CTRL+U
Make text small capital letters, or return small capital letters to upper and lower case	CTRL+SHIFT+K
Open the **Font** dialog	CTRL+SHIFT+F
Copy formatting	CTRL+SHIFT+C
Paste formatting	CTRL+SHIFT+V
Turn **Special Characters** on or off	CTRL+SHIFT+Y
Return character formatting to the current text style	CTRL+SPACEBAR
Apply or remove subscript formatting	CTRL+=
Apply or remove superscript formatting	CTRL+SHIFT+=
Increase space between letters in a word (kerning)	CTRL+SHIFT+]
Decrease space between letters in a word (kerning)	CTRL+SHIFT+[
Increase font size by 1.0 point	CTRL+]
Decrease font size by 1.0 point	CTRL+[
Increase to the next size in the **Font Size** box	CTRL+SHIFT+>
Decrease to the next size in the **Font Size** box	CTRL+SHIFT+<
Center a paragraph	CTRL+E
Align a paragraph on the left	CTRL+L

Align a paragraph on the right	CTRL+R
Align a paragraph on both sides (justified)	CTRL+J
Distribute a paragraph evenly horizontally	CTRL+SHIFT+D
Set newspaper alignment for a paragraph (East Asian languages only)	CTRL+SHIFT+J
Display the **Hyphenation** dialog box	CTRL+SHIFT+H
Insert the current time	ALT+SHIFT+T
Insert the current date	ALT+SHIFT+D
Insert the current page number	ALT+SHIFT+P
Prevent the word from getting hyphenated if it occurs at the end of a line	CTRL+SHIFT+0 (zero)

Copy text formats

TASK	SHORTCUT
Copy formatting from the selected text	CTRL+SHIFT+C
Apply copied formatting to text	CTRL+SHIFT+V

Copy, cut, paste or delete text or objects

TASK	SHORTCUT	
Copy the selected text or object	CTRL+C CTRL+INSERT	or
Cut the selected text or object	CTRL+X SHIFT+DELETE	or
Paste text or an object	CTRL+V SHIFT+INSERT	or
Delete the selected object	DELETE CTRL+SHIFT+X	or

Undo or redo an action

TASK	SHORTCUT
Undo what you last did	CTRL+Z or ALT+BACKSPACE
Redo what you last did	CTRL+Y or F4

Nudge an object

TASK	SHORTCUT
Nudge a selected object up, down, left, or right	Arrow keys
If the selected object has a cursor in its text, nudge the selected object up, down, left, or right	ALT+arrow keys

Layer Objects

TASK	SHORTCUT
Bring object to front	ALT+F6
Send object to back	ALT+SHIFT+F6

Snap Objects

TASK	SHORTCUT
Turn **Snap to Guides** on or off	F10, SHIFT+R, SHIFT+S, SHIFT+M

Select or Group Objects

TASK	SHORTCUT
Select all objects on the page (If your cursor is in a text box, this selects all the text in a story)	CTRL+A
Group selected objects, or ungroup grouped objects	CTRL+SHIFT+G
Clear the selection from selected text	ESC

Clear the selection from a selected object	ESC
Select the object within the group — if that object contains selected text	ESC

Work With Pages

Select or insert pages

If your publication is in Two-Page Spread view, these commands apply to the selected two-page spread. Otherwise, these apply only to the selected page.

TASK	SHORTCUT
Display the **Go To Page** dialog box	F5 or CTRL+G
Insert a page or a two-page spread. If you are creating a newsletter, it opens the **Insert publication type Pages** dialog box	CTRL+SHIFT+N
Insert duplicate page after the selected page	CTRL+SHIFT+U

Move between pages

TASK	SHORTCUT
Display the **Go To Page** dialog box.	F5 or CTRL+G
Go to the next page	CTRL+PAGE DOWN
Go to the previous page	CTRL+PAGE UP
Switch between the current page and the master page	CTRL+M

Use the Master Page

TASK	SHORTCUT
Switch between the current page and the master page.	CTRL+M

Show or Hide Boundaries or Guides

TASK	SHORTCUT
Turn **Boundaries** on or off.	CTRL+SHIFT+O
Turn **Horizontal Baseline Guides** on or off (not available in web view)	CTRL+F7
Turn **Vertical Baseline Guides** on or off (East Asian languages only—not available in web view)	CTRL+SHIFT+F7

Zoom

TASK	SHORTCUT
Switch between the current view and the actual size	F9
Zoom to full page view	CTRL+SHIFT+L

Printing

Using Print Preview

These keyboard shortcuts are available when you're in **Print** view and affect the print preview pane.

TASK	SHORTCUT
Switch between the current view and the actual size	F9
Scroll up or down	UP ARROW or DOWN ARROW

Scroll left or right	LEFT ARROW or RIGHT ARROW
Scroll up in large increments	PAGE UP or CTRL+UP ARROW
Scroll down in large increments	PAGE DOWN or CTRL+DOWN ARROW
Scroll left in large increments	CTRL+LEFT ARROW
Scroll right in large increments	CTRL+RIGHT ARROW
Scroll to the upper left corner of the page	HOME
Scroll to the lower right corner of the page	END
Display the **Go To Page** dialog box	F5 or CTRL+G
Go to the previous page	CTRL+PAGE UP
Go to the next page	CTRL+PAGE DOWN
Go to the next window (if you have multiple publications open)	CTRL+F6
Exit **Print Preview** and display the **Print** view	CTRL+P
Exit **Print Preview**	ESC

Print a publication

TASK	SHORTCUT
Open the **Print** dialog view.	CTRL+P

Work with web pages and email

Insert hyperlinks

TASK	SHORTCUT
Display the **Insert Hyperlink** dialog box (make sure your cursor is in a text box)	CTRL+K

Send e-mail

After you choose **Send as Message** (**File** > **Share** > **Email**), you can use the following keyboard shortcuts.

Important: Outlook needs to be open before you can send email messages. If Outlook isn't open, the message will be stored in your **Outbox** folder.

TASK	SHORTCUT
Send the current page or publication	ALT+S
Open the **Address Book** (cursor must be in the message header)	CTRL+SHIFT+B
Open the **Design Checker** (cursor must be in the message header)	ALT+K
Check the names on the **To**, **Cc**, and **Bcc** lines (cursor must be in the message header)	CTRL+K
Open the **Address Book** with the **To** box selected (cursor must be in the message header)	ALT+. (period)
Open the **Address Book** with the **Cc** box selected (cursor must be in the message header)	ALT+C
Open the **Address Book** with the **Bcc** box selected (cursor must be in the message header and the **Bcc** field must be visible)	ALT+B
Go to the **Subject** box	ALT+J

Open the Outlook **Message Options** dialog box	ALT+P
Open the **Custom** dialog box to create an email message flag (cursor must be in the email message header)	CTRL+SHIFT+G
Move the cursor to the next field in the email message header (cursor must be in the email message header)	TAB
Move the cursor to the previous field in the email message header	SHIFT+TAB
Alternate between the insertion point in the email message header and the **Send** button in the **Mailing** toolbar	CTRL+TAB
Open the **Address Book** when the cursor is in the e-mail message header	CTRL+SHIFT+B

Automate Tasks

Work with macros

TASK	SHORTCUT
Display the **Macros** dialog box.	ALT+F8

Work with Visual Basic

TASK	SHORTCUT
Display the Visual Basic editor	ALT+F11

CHAPTER 4.

Keyboard Shortcuts In SharePoint 2013.

Definition of Program: Microsoft SharePoint is a web application that goes with Microsoft office bundle, developed and sold by Microsoft Corporation.

The following list of shortcut keys will help you to excel in Microsoft SharePoint.

All Pages

These keyboard shortcuts apply to all pages.

TASK	SHORTCUT
Turn More Accessible Mode on or off.	TAB (Press repeatedly, immediately after you open the page in a browser.)
Expand menus, such as the drop-down menu for a list item.	SHIFT+ENTER
Move to different options in a drop down list, such as the **Search Scope** menu next to the **Search** box at the top of some pages.	ALT+DOWN ARROW

Edit Rich Text

Use rich text editing

Rich text editing is available in several locations, such the **Insert** tab when you edit a page on a site.

TASK	SHORTCUT
Apply or remove bold formatting from the selected text.	CTRL+B
Apply or remove italic formatting from the selected text.	CTRL+I
Apply or remove the underline from the selected text.	CTRL+U
Remove a paragraph indent from the left.	CTRL+SHIFT+M
Indent a paragraph from the left.	CTRL+ M
Delete the selection without adding it on the Clipboard.	DELETE
Switch between inserting and overwriting text.	INSERT
Delete the selection, or if there is no selection, the character in front of the cursor.	BACKSPACE
Delete all of the word in front of the cursor, but not the previous space.	CTRL+BACKSPACE
Insert a new line (but not inside the HTML Paragraph element <P>).	SHIFT+ENTER

List Or Library Page

The following keyboard shortcuts are available in OneDrive for Business or in a SharePoint list or library.

TASK	SHORTCUT
Create a document.	Alt + N.

	Alt + N opens a shortcut menu that lists the types of documents that you can create: Microsoft Word 2013, Excel, PowerPoint, or OneNote. You can also add a new folder to the library.
Upload a document.	ALT + U opens a dialog box where you can browse for a file to upload.
Edit a page in Datasheet view.	In a SharePoint list, select a list item and then TAB to find the **edit** command.
Create a folder.	ALT + N, then Tab to find **New folder** on the shortcut menu.

Survey Page

TASK	SHORTCUT
Activate the **Actions** menu.	ALT+C (To open the menu, press SHIFT+ENTER. To select a command, press DOWN ARROW.)
Activate the **Respond to this Survey** button.	ALT+N
Activate the **Export Results to spreadsheet** command. This command is located on the **Actions** menu.	ALT+C (To open the menu, press SHIFT+ENTER. To select a command, press DOWN ARROW.)
Activate the **Show a graphical summary of responses** link.	ALT+R
Select the **Save and Close** button in a form for editing a survey response, .	ALT+S
Activate the **Show all responses** link.	ALT+U

Activate the **Settings** menu.	ALT+I
Activate the **Next Page** button.	ALT+N

Getting Help

To open the Help window, Tab to the "?" (question mark) image, and then press Enter to open a shortcut menu. The Help window displays a list of links to help and how-to topics that are related to the active page.

CHAPTER 5

Keyboard Shortcuts In Word 2013.

Definition of Program: Microsoft Word is a word processing program designed in 1983 by Microsoft Corporation. It allows users to create and modify simple and sophisticated documents.

The following list of shortcut keys will help you to excel in Microsoft Word.

Frequently Used Shortcuts

This table shows the most frequently used shortcuts in Microsoft Word.

TASK	SHORTCUT
Go to "Tell me what you want to do"	ALT+Q
Open	CTRL+O
Save	CTRL+S
Close	CTRL+W
Cut	CTRL+X
Copy	CTRL+C
Paste	CTRL+V
Select all	CTRL+A
Bold	CTRL+B
Italic	CTRL+I
Underline	CTRL+U
Decrease font size 1 point	CTRL+[

Increase font size 1 point	CTRL+]
Center text	CTRL+E
Left align text	CTRL+L
Right align text	CTRL+R
Cancel	Esc
Undo	CTRL+Z
Re-do	CTRL+Y
Zoom	ALT+W, Q, then tab in Zoom dialog box to the value you want.

Navigate The Ribbon With Only The Keyboard.

The ribbon is the strip at the top of Word, organized by tabs. Each tab displays a different ribbon. Ribbons are made up of groups, and each group includes one or more commands. Every command in Word can be accessed by using shortcut.

Note: Add-ins and other programs may add new tabs to the ribbon and may provide access keys for those tabs.

There are two ways to navigate the tabs in the ribbon:

- To go to the ribbon, press Alt, and then, to move between tabs, use the Right Arrow and Left Arrow keys.
- To go directly to a specific tab on the ribbon, use one of the access keys

TASK	SHORTCUT
To use Backstage view, open the **File** page.	ALT+F

To use themes, colors, and effects, such as page borders, open the **Design** tab.	ALT+G
To use common formatting commands, paragraph styles, or to use the Find tool. open **Home** tab.	ALT+H
To manage Mail Merge tasks, or to work with envelopes and labels, open **Mailings** tab .	ALT+M
To insert tables, pictures and shapes, headers, or text boxes, open **Insert** tab.	ALT+N
To work with page margins, page orientation, indentation, and spacing, open **Layout** tab.	ALT+P
To type a search term for Help content, open "Tell me" box on ribbon.	ALT+Q, then enter the search term
To use Spell Check, set proofing languages, or to track and review changes to your document, open the **Review** tab.	ALT+R
To add a table of contents, footnotes, or a table of citations, open the **References** tab.	ALT+S
To choose a document view or mode, such as Read Mode or Outline view, open the **View** tab. You can also set Zoom magnification and manage multiple windows of documents.	ALT+W

Use commands on a ribbon with the keyboard

- To move to the list of ribbon tabs, press Alt; to go directly to a tab, press a keyboard shortcut.

- To move into the ribbon, press the Down Arrow key. (JAWS refers to this action as a move to the lower ribbon.)
- To move between commands, press the Tab key or Shift+Tab.
- To move in the group that's currently selected, press the Down Arrow key.
- To move between groups on a ribbon, press Ctrl+Right Arrow or Ctrl+Left Arrow.
- Controls on the ribbon are activated in different ways, depending upon the type of control:
  - If the selected command is a button, to activate it, press SPACEBAR or ENTER.
  - If the selected command is a split button (that is, a button that opens a menu of additional options), to activate it, press Alt+Down Arrow. Tab through the options. To select the current option, press SPACEBAR or ENTER.
  - If the selected command is a list (such as the Font list), to open the list, press the Down Arrow key. Then, to move between items, use the Up Arrow or Down Arrow key.
  - If the selected command is a gallery, to select the command, press SPACEBAR or ENTER. Then, tab through the items.

Tip: In galleries with more than one row of items, the Tab key moves from the beginning to the end of the current row and, when it reaches the end of the row, it moves to the beginning of the next one. Pressing the Right Arrow key at the end of the current row moves back to the beginning of the current row.

Use access keys when you can see the KeyTips

To use access keys:

1. Press ALT.
2. Press the letter shown in the square KeyTip that appears over the ribbon command that you want to use.

Depending on which letter you press, you may be shown additional KeyTips. For example, if you press ALT+F, the Office Backstage opens on the Info page which has a different set of KeyTips. If you then press ALT again, KeyTips for navigating on this page appear.

Change The Keyboard Focus By Using The Keyboard Without Using The Mouse

The following table lists some ways to move the keyboard focus when using only the keyboard.

TASK	SHORTCUT
Select the active tab of the ribbon and activate the access keys.	ALT or F10. Use access keys or arrow keys to move to a different tab.
Move the focus to commands on the ribbon.	TAB or SHIFT+TAB
Move the focus to each command on the ribbon, forward or backward, respectively.	TAB or SHIFT+TAB
Move down, up, left, or right, respectively, among the items on the ribbon.	DOWN ARROW, UP ARROW, LEFT ARROW, or RIGHT ARROW
Expand or collapse the ribbon.	CTRL+F1
Display the shortcut menu for a selected item.	SHIFT+F10

Move the focus to a different pane of the window, such as the Format Picture pane, the Grammar pane, or the Selection pane.	F6
Activate a selected command or control on the ribbon.	SPACEBAR or ENTER
Open a selected menu or gallery on the ribbon.	SPACEBAR or ENTER
Finish modifying a value in a control on the ribbon, and move focus back to the document.	ENTER

Keyboard Shortcut Reference For Microsoft Word.

Create and edit documents

Create, view, and save documents

TASK	SHORTCUT
Create a new document.	CTRL+N
Open a document.	CTRL+O
Close a document.	CTRL+W
Split the document window.	ALT+CTRL+S
Remove the document window split.	ALT+SHIFT+C or ALT+CTRL+S
Save a document.	CTRL+S

Work with Web content

TASK	SHORTCUT
Insert a hyperlink.	CTRL+K
Go back one page.	ALT+LEFT ARROW
Go forward one page.	ALT+RIGHT ARROW

Refresh.	F9

Print and preview documents

TASK	SHORTCUT
Print a document.	CTRL+P
Switch to print preview.	ALT+CTRL+I
Move around the preview page when zoomed in.	Arrow keys
Move by one preview page when zoomed out.	PAGE UP or PAGE DOWN
Move to the first preview page when zoomed out.	CTRL+HOME
Move to the last preview page when zoomed out.	CTRL+END

Check spelling and review changes in a document

TASK	SHORTCUT
Insert a comment (in the Revision task pane).	ALT+R, C
Turn change tracking on or off.	CTRL+SHIFT+E
Close the Reviewing Pane if it is open.	ALT+SHIFT+C
Select Review tab on ribbon.	ALT+R, then DOWN ARROW to move to commands on this tab.
Select Spelling & Grammar	ALT+R, S

Find, replace, and go to specific items in the document

TASK	SHORTCUT
Open the search box in the **Navigation** task pane.	CTRL+F
Replace text, specific formatting, and special items.	CTRL+H

Go to a page, bookmark, footnote, table, comment, graphic, or other location.	CTRL+G
Switch between the last four places that you have edited.	ALT+CTRL+Z

Move around in a document using the keyboard

TASK	SHORTCUT
One character to the left	LEFT ARROW
One character to the right	RIGHT ARROW
One word to the left	CTRL+LEFT ARROW
One word to the right	CTRL+RIGHT ARROW
One paragraph up	CTRL+UP ARROW
One paragraph down	CTRL+DOWN ARROW
One cell to the left (in a table)	SHIFT+TAB
One cell to the right (in a table)	TAB
Up one line	UP ARROW
Down one line	DOWN ARROW
To the end of a line	END
To the beginning of a line	HOME
To the top of the window	ALT+CTRL+PAGE UP
To the end of the window	ALT+CTRL+PAGE DOWN
Up one screen (scrolling)	PAGE UP
Down one screen (scrolling)	PAGE DOWN
To the top of the next page	CTRL+PAGE DOWN
To the top of the previous page	CTRL+PAGE UP
To the end of a document	CTRL+END
To the beginning of a document	CTRL+HOME
To a previous revision	SHIFT+F5
After opening a document, to the location you were working in	SHIFT+F5

when the document was last closed	

Insert or mark Table of Contents, footnotes, and citations

TASK	SHORTCUT
Mark a table of contents entry.	ALT+SHIFT+O
Mark a table of authorities entry (citation).	ALT+SHIFT+I
Mark an index entry.	ALT+SHIFT+X
Insert a footnote.	ALT+CTRL+F
Insert an endnote.	ALT+CTRL+D
Go to next footnote (in Word 2016).	ALT+SHIFT+>
Go to previous footnote (in Word 2016).	ALT+SHIFT+<
Go to "Tell me what you want to do" and Smart Lookup (in Word 2016).	ALT+Q

Work with documents in different views

Word offers several different views of a document. Each view makes it easier to do certain tasks. For example, Read Mode enables you to present two pages of the document side by side, and to use an arrow navigation to move to the next page.

Switch to another view of the document

TASK	SHORTCUT
Switch to Read Mode view	ALT+W, F
Switch to Print Layout view.	ALT+CTRL+P
Switch to Outline view.	ALT+CTRL+O
Switch to Draft view.	ALT+CTRL+N

Work with headings in Outline view

These shortcuts only apply if a document is in Outline view.

TASK	SHORTCUT
Promote a paragraph.	ALT+SHIFT+LEFT ARROW
Demote a paragraph.	ALT+SHIFT+RIGHT ARROW
Demote to body text.	CTRL+SHIFT+N
Move selected paragraphs up.	ALT+SHIFT+UP ARROW
Move selected paragraphs down.	ALT+SHIFT+DOWN ARROW
Expand text under a heading.	ALT+SHIFT+PLUS SIGN
Collapse text under a heading.	ALT+SHIFT+MINUS SIGN
Expand or collapse all text or headings.	ALT+SHIFT+A
Hide or display character formatting.	The slash (/) key on the numeric keypad
Show the first line of text or all text.	ALT+SHIFT+L
Show all headings with the Heading 1 style.	ALT+SHIFT+1
Show all headings up to Heading n.	ALT+SHIFT+n
Insert a tab character.	CTRL+TAB

Navigate in Read Mode view

TASK	SHORTCUT
Go to beginning of document.	HOME
Go to end of document.	END
Go to page n.	n (n is the page number you want to go to), ENTER
Exit Read mode.	ESC

Edit and move text and graphics

Select text and graphics

Select text by holding down SHIFT and using the arrow keys to move the cursor

Extend a selection

TASK	SHORTCUT
Turn extend mode on.	F8
Select the nearest character.	F8, and then press LEFT ARROW or RIGHT ARROW
Increase the size of a selection.	F8 (press once to select a word, twice to select a sentence, and so on)
Reduce the size of a selection.	SHIFT+F8
Turn extend mode off.	ESC
Extend a selection one character to the right.	SHIFT+RIGHT ARROW
Extend a selection one character to the left.	SHIFT+LEFT ARROW
Extend a selection to the end of a word.	CTRL+SHIFT+RIGHT ARROW
Extend a selection to the beginning of a word.	CTRL+SHIFT+LEFT ARROW
Extend a selection to the end of a line.	SHIFT+END

Extend a selection to the beginning of a line.	SHIFT+HOME
Extend a selection one line down.	SHIFT+DOWN ARROW
Extend a selection one line up.	SHIFT+UP ARROW
Extend a selection to the end of a paragraph.	CTRL+SHIFT+DOWN ARROW
Extend a selection to the beginning of a paragraph.	CTRL+SHIFT+UP ARROW
Extend a selection one screen down.	SHIFT+PAGE DOWN
Extend a selection one screen up.	SHIFT+PAGE UP
Extend a selection to the beginning of a document.	CTRL+SHIFT+HOME
Extend a selection to the end of a document.	CTRL+SHIFT+END
Extend a selection to the end of a window.	ALT+CTRL+SHIFT+PAGE DOWN
Extend a selection to include the entire document.	CTRL+A
Select a vertical block of text.	CTRL+SHIFT+F8, and then use the arrow keys; press ESC to cancel selection mode
Extend a selection to a specific	F8+arrow keys; press ESC to cancel selection mode

location in a document.	

Delete text and graphics

TASK	SHORTCUT
Delete one character to the left.	BACKSPACE
Delete one word to the left.	CTRL+BACKSPACE
Delete one character to the right.	DELETE
Delete one word to the right.	CTRL+DELETE
Cut selected text to the Office Clipboard.	CTRL+X
Undo the last action.	CTRL+Z
Cut to the Spike. (Spike is a feature that allows you to collect groups of text from different locations and paste them in another location).	CTRL+F3

Copy and move text and graphics

TASK	SHORTCUT
Open the Office Clipboard	Press ALT+H to move to the **Home** tab, and then press F,O.
Copy selected text or graphics to the Office Clipboard.	CTRL+C
Cut selected text or graphics to the Office Clipboard.	CTRL+X
Paste the most recent addition or pasted item from the Office Clipboard.	CTRL+V
Move text or graphics once.	F2 (then move the cursor and press ENTER)
Copy text or graphics once.	SHIFT+F2 (then move the cursor and press ENTER)

When text or an object is selected, open the **Create New Building Block** dialog box.	ALT+F3
When the building block — for example, a SmartArt graphic — is selected, display the shortcut menu that is associated with it.	SHIFT+F10
Cut to the Spike.	CTRL+F3
Paste the Spike contents.	CTRL+SHIFT+F3
Copy the header or footer used in the previous section of the document.	ALT+SHIFT+R

Edit and navigate tables

Select text and graphics in a table

TASK	SHORTCUT
Select the next cell's contents.	TAB
Select the preceding cell's contents.	SHIFT+TAB
Extend a selection to adjacent cells.	Hold down SHIFT and press an arrow key repeatedly
Select a column.	Use the arrow keys to move to the column's top or bottom cell, and then do one of the following:

	• Press SHIFT+ALT+PAGE DOWN to select the column from top to bottom. • Press SHIFT+ALT+PAGE UP to select the column from bottom to top.
Select an entire row	Use arrow keys to move to end of the row, either the first cell (leftmost) in the row or to the last cell (rightmost) in the row. • From the first cell in the row, press SHIFT+ALT+END to select the row from left to right. • From the last cell in the row, press SHIFT+ALT+HOME to select the row from right to left.
Extend a selection (or block).	CTRL+SHIFT+F8, and then use the arrow keys; press ESC to cancel selection mode
Select an entire table.	ALT+5 on the numeric keypad (with NUM LOCK off)

Move around in a table

TASK	SHORTCUT
To the next cell in a row	TAB
To the previous cell in a row	SHIFT+TAB
To the first cell in a row	ALT+HOME
To the last cell in a row	ALT+END
To the first cell in a column	ALT+PAGE UP
To the last cell in a column	ALT+PAGE DOWN

To the previous row	UP ARROW
To the next row	DOWN ARROW
Row up	ALT+SHIFT+UP ARROW
Row down	ALT+SHIFT+DOWN ARROW

Insert paragraphs and tab characters in a table

TASK	SHORTCUT
New paragraphs in a cell	ENTER
Tab characters in a cell	CTRL+TAB

Format characters and paragraphs

Format characters

TASK	SHORTCUT
Open the **Font** dialog box to change the formatting of characters.	CTRL+D
Change the case of letters.	SHIFT+F3
Format all letters as capitals.	CTRL+SHIFT+A
Apply bold formatting.	CTRL+B
Apply an underline.	CTRL+U
Underline words but not spaces.	CTRL+SHIFT+W
Double-underline text.	CTRL+SHIFT+D
Apply hidden text formatting.	CTRL+SHIFT+H
Apply italic formatting.	CTRL+I
Format letters as small capitals.	CTRL+SHIFT+K
Apply subscript formatting (automatic spacing).	CTRL+EQUAL SIGN
Apply superscript formatting (automatic spacing).	CTRL+SHIFT+PLUS SIGN
Remove manual character formatting.	CTRL+SPACEBAR

Change the selection to the Symbol font.	CTRL+SHIFT+Q

Change or re-size the font

TASK	SHORTCUT
Open the **Font** dialog box to change the font.	CTRL+SHIFT+F
Increase the font size.	CTRL+SHIFT+>
Decrease the font size.	CTRL+SHIFT+<
Increase the font size by 1 point.	CTRL+]
Decrease the font size by 1 point.	CTRL+[

Copy formatting

TASK	SHORTCUT
Copy formatting from text.	CTRL+SHIFT+C
Apply copied formatting to text.	CTRL+SHIFT+V

Change paragraph alignment

TASK	SHORTCUT
Switch a paragraph between centered and left-aligned.	CTRL+E
Switch a paragraph between justified and left-aligned.	CTRL+J
Switch a paragraph between right-aligned and left-aligned.	CTRL+R
Left align a paragraph.	CTRL+L
Indent a paragraph from the left.	CTRL+M
Remove a paragraph indent from the left.	CTRL+SHIFT+M
Create a hanging indent.	CTRL+T
Reduce a hanging indent.	CTRL+SHIFT+T
Remove paragraph formatting.	CTRL+Q

Copy and review text formats

TASK	SHORTCUT
Display nonprinting characters.	CTRL+SHIFT+* (asterisk on numeric keypad does not work)

Review text formatting.	SHIFT+F1 (then click the text with the formatting you want to review)
Copy formats.	CTRL+SHIFT+C
Paste formats.	CTRL+SHIFT+V

Set line spacing

TASK	SHORTCUT
Single-space lines.	CTRL+1
Double-space lines.	CTRL+2
Set 1.5-line spacing.	CTRL+5
Add or remove one line space preceding a paragraph.	CTRL+0 (zero)

Apply Styles to paragraphs

TASK	SHORTCUT
Open **Apply Styles** task pane.	CTRL+SHIFT+S
Open **Styles** task pane.	ALT+CTRL+SHIFT+S
Start AutoFormat.	ALT+CTRL+K
Apply the Normal style.	CTRL+SHIFT+N
Apply the Heading 1 style.	ALT+CTRL+1
Apply the Heading 2 style.	ALT+CTRL+2
Apply the Heading 3 style.	ALT+CTRL+3

To close the Styles task pane

1. If the **Styles** task pane is not selected, press F6 to select it.
2. Press CTRL+SPACEBAR.
3. Use the arrow keys to select **Close**, and then press ENTER.

Insert special characters

TASK	SHORTCUT
A field	CTRL+F9
A line break	SHIFT+ENTER
A page break	CTRL+ENTER

A column break	CTRL+SHIFT+ENTER
An em dash	ALT+CTRL+MINUS SIGN (on the numeric keypad)
An en dash	CTRL+MINUS SIGN (on the numeric keypad)
An optional hyphen	CTRL+HYPHEN
A nonbreaking hyphen	CTRL+SHIFT+HYPHEN
A nonbreaking space	CTRL+SHIFT+SPACEBAR
The copyright symbol	ALT+CTRL+C
The registered trademark symbol	ALT+CTRL+R
The trademark symbol	ALT+CTRL+T
An ellipsis	ALT+CTRL+PERIOD
A single opening quotation mark	CTRL+`(single quotation mark), `(single quotation mark)
A single closing quotation mark	CTRL+' (single quotation mark), ' (single quotation mark)
Double opening quotation marks	CTRL+` (single quotation mark), SHIFT+' (single quotation mark)
Double closing quotation marks	CTRL+' (single quotation mark), SHIFT+' (single quotation mark)
An AutoText entry	ENTER (after you type the first few characters of the AutoText entry name and when the ScreenTip appears)

Insert characters by using character codes

TASK	SHORTCUT
Insert the Unicode character for the specified Unicode (hexadecimal) character code. For example, to insert the euro currency symbol (€), type **20AC**, and then hold down ALT and press X.	The character code, ALT+X
Find out the Unicode character code for the selected character	ALT+X
Insert the ANSI character for the specified ANSI (decimal) character code. For example, to insert the euro currency symbol, hold down ALT and press 0128 on the numeric keypad.	ALT+the character code (on the numeric keypad)

Insert and edit objects

Insert an object

1. Press ALT, N, J, and then J to open the **Object** dialog box.
2. Do one of the following.
   - Press DOWN ARROW to select an object type, and then press ENTER to create an object.
   - Press CTRL+TAB to switch to the **Create from File** tab, press TAB, and then type the file name of the object that you want to insert or browse to the file.

Edit an object

1. With the cursor positioned to the left of the object in your document, select the object by pressing SHIFT+RIGHT ARROW.
2. Press SHIFT+F10.
3. Press the TAB key to get to **Object name**, press ENTER, and then press ENTER again.

Insert SmartArt graphics

1. Press and release ALT, N, and then M to select **SmartArt**.
2. Press the arrow keys to select the type of graphic that you want.
3. Press TAB, and then press the arrow keys to select the graphic that you want to insert.
4. Press ENTER.

Insert WordArt

1. Press and release ALT, N, and then W to select **WordArt**.
2. Press the arrow keys to select the WordArt style that you want, and then press ENTER.
3. Type the text that you want.
4. Press ESC to select the WordArt object, and then use the arrow keys to move the object.
5. Press ESC again to return to return to the document.

Mail merge and fields

Note: You must press ALT+M, or click **Mailings**, to use these keyboard shortcuts.

Perform a mail merge

TASK	SHORTCUT
Preview a mail merge.	ALT+SHIFT+K
Merge a document.	ALT+SHIFT+N
Print the merged document.	ALT+SHIFT+M
Edit a mail-merge data document.	ALT+SHIFT+E
Insert a merge field.	ALT+SHIFT+F

Work with fields

TASK	SHORTCUT
Insert a DATE field.	ALT+SHIFT+D
Insert a LISTNUM field.	ALT+CTRL+L
Insert a PAGE field.	ALT+SHIFT+P
Insert a TIME field.	ALT+SHIFT+T
Insert an empty field.	CTRL+F9
Update linked information in a Microsoft Word source document.	CTRL+SHIFT+F7
Update selected fields.	F9
Unlink a field.	CTRL+SHIFT+F9
Switch between a selected field code and its result.	SHIFT+F9
Switch between all field codes and their results.	ALT+F9
Run GOTOBUTTON or MACROBUTTON from the field that displays the field results.	ALT+SHIFT+F9
Go to the next field.	F11
Go to the previous field.	SHIFT+F11
Lock a field.	CTRL+F11
Unlock a field.	CTRL+SHIFT+F11

Language Bar

Set proofing language

Every document has a default language, typically the same default language as your computer's operating system. But If your document also contains words or phrases in a different language, it's a good idea to set the proofing language for those words. This not only makes it possible to check spelling and grammar for those phrases, it makes it possible for assistive technologies like screen readers to handle them.

TASK	SHORTCUT
Open the **Set Proofing Language** dialog box	ALT+R, U, L
Review list of proofing languages	DOWN ARROW
Set default languages	ALT+R, L

Turn on East Asian Input Method Editors

TASK	SHORTCUT
Turn Japanese Input Method Editor (IME) on 101 keyboard on or off.	ALT+~
Turn Korean Input Method Editor (IME) on 101 keyboard on or off.	Right ALT
Turn Chinese Input Method Editor (IME) on 101 keyboard on or off.	CTRL+SPACEBAR

Function Key Reference.

Function keys

TASK	SHORTCUT
Get Help or visit Office.com.	F1
Move text or graphics.	F2
Repeat the last action.	F4

Choose the **Go To** command (**Home** tab).	F5
Go to the next pane or frame.	F6
Choose the **Spelling** command (**Review** tab).	F7
Extend a selection.	F8
Update the selected fields.	F9
Show KeyTips.	F10
Go to the next field.	F11
Choose the **Save As** command.	F12

SHIFT+Function Keys

TASK	SHORTCUT
Start context-sensitive Help or reveal formatting.	SHIFT+F1
Copy text.	SHIFT+F2
Change the case of letters.	SHIFT+F3
Repeat a **Find** or **Go To** action.	SHIFT+F4
Move to the last change.	SHIFT+F5
Go to the previous pane or frame (after pressing F6).	SHIFT+F6
Choose the **Thesaurus** command (**Review** tab, **Proofing** group).	SHIFT+F7
Reduce the size of a selection.	SHIFT+F8
Switch between a field code and its result.	SHIFT+F9
Display a shortcut menu.	SHIFT+F10
Go to the previous field.	SHIFT+F11
Choose the **Save** command.	SHIFT+F12

CTRL+Function Keys

TASK	SHORTCUT
Expand or collapse the ribbon.	CTRL+F1

Choose the **Print Preview** command.	CTRL+F2
Cut to the Spike.	CTRL+F3
Close the window.	CTRL+F4
Go to the next window.	CTRL+F6
Insert an empty field.	CTRL+F9
Maximize the document window.	CTRL+F10
Lock a field.	CTRL+F11
Choose the **Open** command.	CTRL+F12

CTRL+SHIFT+Function Keys

TASK	SHORTCUT
Insert the contents of the Spike.	CTRL+SHIFT+F3
Edit a bookmark.	CTRL+SHIFT+F5
Go to the previous window.	CTRL+SHIFT+F6
Update linked information in a Word source document.	CTRL+SHIFT+F7
Extend a selection or block.	CTRL+SHIFT+F8, and then press an arrow key
Unlink a field.	CTRL+SHIFT+F9
Unlock a field.	CTRL+SHIFT+F11
Choose the **Print** command.	CTRL+SHIFT+F12

ALT+Function keys

TASK	SHORTCUT
Go to the next field.	ALT+F1
Create a new **Building Block**.	ALT+F3
Exit Word.	ALT+F4
Restore the program window size.	ALT+F5

Move from an open dialog box back to the document, for dialog boxes that support this behavior.	ALT+F6
Find the next misspelling or grammatical error.	ALT+F7
Run a macro.	ALT+F8
Switch between all field codes and their results.	ALT+F9
Display the **Selection** task pane.	ALT+F10
Display Microsoft Visual Basic code.	ALT+F11

ALT+SHIFT+Function keys

TASK	SHORTCUT
Go to the previous field.	ALT+SHIFT+F1
Choose the **Save** command.	ALT+SHIFT+F2
Run GOTOBUTTON or MACROBUTTON from the field that displays the field results.	ALT+SHIFT+F9
Display a menu or message for an available action.	ALT+SHIFT+F10
Choose **Table of Contents** button in the Table of Contents container when the container is active.	ALT+SHIFT+F12

CTRL+ALT+Function keys

TASK	SHORTCUT
Display Microsoft System Information.	CTRL+ALT+F1
Choose the **Open** command.	CTRL+ALT+F2

CHAPTER 6.

Keyboard Shortcuts In Excel 2013.

Definition of Program: Microsoft Excel is an electronic spreadsheet program that enables its users to create, organize, format, and calculate data. It was first released for Macintosh in the year 1985 and later on released for Windows in 1987.

The following list of shortcut keys will help you to excel in Microsoft Excel.

Keyboard Access To The Ribbon

If you're new to the ribbon, the information in this section can help you understand the ribbon's keyboard shortcut model. The ribbon comes with new shortcuts, called **Key Tips**. To make the Key Tips appear, press Alt.

To display a tab on the ribbon, press the key for the tab— for example, press the letter N for the **Insert** tab or M for the **Formulas** tab. This makes all the Key Tip badges for that tab's buttons appear. Then, press the key for the button you want.

Will my old shortcuts still work?

Keyboard shortcuts that begin with Ctrl will still work in Microsoft Excel 2013. For example, Ctrl+C still copies to the clipboard, and Ctrl+V still pastes from the clipboard.

Most of the old Alt+ menu shortcuts still work, too. However, you need to know the full shortcut from memory — there are no screen reminders of what letters to press. For example, try pressing Alt, and then press one of the old menu keys E (Edit), V (View), I (Insert), and so on. A box pops up saying you're using an access key from an earlier version of Microsoft Office. If you know the entire key sequence, go ahead and initiate the command. If you don't know the sequence, press Esc and use Key Tip badges instead.

Ctrl Combination Shortcut Keys

SHORTCUT	TASK
Ctrl+PgDn	Switches between worksheet tabs, from left-to-right.
Ctrl+PgUp	Switches between worksheet tabs, from right-to-left.
Ctrl+Shift+&	Applies the outline border to the selected cells.
Ctrl+Shift_	Removes the outline border from the selected cells.
Ctrl+Shift+~	Applies the General number format.
Ctrl+Shift+$	Applies the Currency format with two decimal places (negative numbers in parentheses).
Ctrl+Shift+%	Applies the Percentage format with no decimal places.
Ctrl+Shift+^	Applies the Scientific number format with two decimal places.
Ctrl+Shift+#	Applies the Date format with the day, month, and year.
Ctrl+Shift+@	Applies the Time format with the hour and minute, and AM or PM.

Ctrl+Shift+!	Applies the Number format with two decimal places, thousands separator, and minus sign (-) for negative values.
Ctrl+Shift+*	Selects the current region around the active cell (the data area enclosed by blank rows and blank columns). In a PivotTable, it selects the entire PivotTable report.
Ctrl+Shift+:	Enters the current time.
Ctrl+Shift+"	Copies the value from the cell above the active cell into the cell or the Formula Bar.
Ctrl+Shift+Plus (+)	Displays the **Insert** dialog box to insert blank cells.
Ctrl+Minus (-)	Displays the **Delete** dialog box to delete the selected cells.
Ctrl+;	Enters the current date.
Ctrl+`	Alternates between displaying cell values and displaying formulas in the worksheet.
Ctrl+'	Copies a formula from the cell above the active cell into the cell or the Formula Bar.
Ctrl+1	Displays the **Format Cells** dialog box.
Ctrl+2	Applies or removes bold formatting.
Ctrl+3	Applies or removes italic formatting.
Ctrl+4	Applies or removes underlining.
Ctrl+5	Applies or removes strikethrough.
Ctrl+6	Alternates between hiding and displaying objects.
Ctrl+8	Displays or hides the outline symbols.
Ctrl+9	Hides the selected rows.
Ctrl+0	Hides the selected columns.

Ctrl+A	Selects the entire worksheet. If the worksheet contains data, Ctrl+A selects the current region. Pressing Ctrl+A a second time selects the entire worksheet. When the insertion point is to the right of a function name in a formula, displays the **Function Arguments** dialog box. Ctrl+Shift+A inserts the argument names and parentheses when the insertion point is to the right of a function name in a formula.
Ctrl+B	Applies or removes bold formatting.
Ctrl+C	Copies the selected cells.
Ctrl+D	Uses the **Fill Down** command to copy the contents and format of the topmost cell of a selected range into the cells below.
Ctrl+E	Adds more values to the active column by using data surrounding that column.
Ctrl+F	Displays the **Find and Replace** dialog box, with the **Find** tab selected. Shift+F5 also displays this tab, while Shift+F4 repeats the last **Find** action. Ctrl+Shift+F opens the **Format Cells** dialog box with the **Font** tab selected.
Ctrl+G	Displays the **Go To** dialog box.

	F5 also displays this dialog box.
Ctrl+H	Displays the **Find and Replace** dialog box, with the **Replace** tab selected.
Ctrl+I	Applies or removes italic formatting.
Ctrl+K	Displays the **Insert Hyperlink** dialog box for new hyperlinks or the **Edit Hyperlink** dialog box for selected existing hyperlinks.
Ctrl+L	Displays the **Create Table** dialog box.
Ctrl+N	Creates a new, blank workbook.
Ctrl+O	Displays the **Open** dialog box to open or find a file. Ctrl+Shift+O selects all cells that contain comments.
Ctrl+P	Displays the **Print** tab in Microsoft Office Backstage view. Ctrl+Shift+P opens the **Format Cells** dialog box with the **Font** tab selected.
Ctrl+Q	Displays the **Quick Analysis** options for your data when you have cells that contain that data selected.
Ctrl+R	Uses the **Fill Right** command to copy the contents and format of the leftmost cell of a selected range into the cells to the right.
Ctrl+S	Saves the active file with its current file name, location, and file format.
Ctrl+T	Displays the **Create Table** dialog box.

Ctrl+U	Applies or removes underlining. Ctrl+Shift+U switches between expanding and collapsing of the formula bar.
Ctrl+V	Inserts the contents of the Clipboard at the insertion point and replaces any selection. Available only after you have cut or copied an object, text, or cell contents. Ctrl+Alt+V displays the **Paste Special** dialog box. Available only after you have cut or copied an object, text, or cell contents on a worksheet or in another program.
Ctrl+W	Closes the selected workbook window.
Ctrl+X	Cuts the selected cells.
Ctrl+Y	Repeats the last command or action, if possible.
Ctrl+Z	Uses the **Undo** command to reverse the last command or to delete the last entry that you typed.

Tip: The Ctrl combinations Ctrl+J and Ctrl+M are currently unassigned shortcuts.

Function Keys

SHORTCUT	TASK
F1	Displays the **Excel Help** task pane. Ctrl+F1 displays or hides the ribbon.

	Alt+F1 creates an embedded chart of the data in the current range. Alt+Shift+F1 inserts a new worksheet.
F2	Edits the active cell and positions the insertion point at the end of the cell contents. It also moves the insertion point into the Formula Bar when editing in a cell is turned off. Shift+F2 adds or edits a cell comment. Ctrl+F2 displays the print preview area on the **Print** tab in the Backstage view.
F3	Displays the **Paste Name** dialog box. Available only if names have been defined in the workbook (**Formulas** tab, **Defined Names** group, **Define Name**). Shift+F3 displays the **Insert Function** dialog box.
F4	Repeats the last command or action, if possible. When a cell reference or range is selected in a formula, F4 cycles through all the various combinations of absolute and relative references. Ctrl+F4 closes the selected workbook window. Alt+F4 closes Excel.
F5	Displays the **Go To** dialog box.

	Ctrl+F5 restores the window size of the selected workbook window.
F6	Switches between the worksheet, ribbon, task pane, and Zoom controls. In a worksheet that has been split (**View** menu, **Manage This Window**, **Freeze Panes**, **Split Window** command), F6 includes the split panes when switching between panes and the ribbon area. Shift+F6 switches between the worksheet, Zoom controls, task pane, and ribbon. Ctrl+F6 switches to the next workbook window when more than one workbook window is open.
F7	Displays the **Spelling** dialog box to check spelling in the active worksheet or selected range. Ctrl+F7 performs the **Move** command on the workbook window when it is not maximized. Use the arrow keys to move the window, and when finished press Enter, or Esc to cancel.
F8	Turns extend mode on or off. In extend mode, **Extended Selection** appears in the status line, and the arrow keys extend the selection. Shift+F8 enables you to add a nonadjacent cell or range to a selection of cells by using the arrow keys.

	Ctrl+F8 performs the **Size** command (on the **Control** menu for the workbook window) when a workbook is not maximized. Alt+F8 displays the **Macro** dialog box to create, run, edit, or delete a macro.
F9	Calculates all worksheets in all open workbooks. Shift+F9 calculates the active worksheet. Ctrl+Alt+F9 calculates all worksheets in all open workbooks, regardless of whether they have changed since the last calculation. Ctrl+Alt+Shift+F9 rechecks dependent formulas, and then calculates all cells in all open workbooks, including cells not marked as needing to be calculated. Ctrl+F9 minimizes a workbook window to an icon.
F10	Turns key tips on or off. (Pressing Alt does the same thing.) Shift+F10 displays the shortcut menu for a selected item. Alt+Shift+F10 displays the menu or message for an Error Checking button. Ctrl+F10 maximizes or restores the selected workbook window.

F11	Creates a chart of the data in the current range in a separate Chart sheet.
	Shift+F11 inserts a new worksheet.
	Alt+F11 opens the Microsoft Visual Basic For Applications Editor, in which you can create a macro by using Visual Basic for Applications (VBA).
F12	Displays the **Save As** dialog box.

Other Useful Shortcut Keys

SHORTCUT	TASK
Alt	Displays the Key Tips (new shortcuts) on the ribbon.
	For example,
	Alt, W, P switches the worksheet to Page Layout view.
	Alt, W, L switches the worksheet to Normal view.
	Alt, W, I switches the worksheet to Page Break Preview view.
Arrow Keys	Move one cell up, down, left, or right in a worksheet.
	Ctrl+Arrow Key moves to the edge of the current data region in a worksheet.
	Shift+Arrow Key extends the selection of cells by one cell.

	Ctrl+Shift+Arrow Key extends the selection of cells to the last nonblank cell in the same column or row as the active cell, or if the next cell is blank, extends the selection to the next nonblank cell. Left Arrow or Right Arrow selects the tab to the left or right when the ribbon is selected. When a submenu is open or selected, these arrow keys switch between the main menu and the submenu. When a ribbon tab is selected, these keys navigate the tab buttons. Down Arrow or Up Arrow selects the next or previous command when a menu or submenu is open. When a ribbon tab is selected, these keys navigate up or down the tab group. In a dialog box, arrow keys move between options in an open drop-down list, or between options in a group of options. Down Arrow or Alt+Down Arrow opens a selected drop-down list.
Backspace	Deletes one character to the left in the Formula Bar. Also clears the content of the active cell. In cell editing mode, it deletes the character to the left of the insertion point.

Delete	Removes the cell contents (data and formulas) from selected cells without affecting cell formats or comments.
	In cell editing mode, it deletes the character to the right of the insertion point.
End	End turns End mode on or off. In End mode, you can press an arrow key to move to the next nonblank cell in the same column or row as the active cell. End mode turns off automatically after pressing the arrow key. Make sure to press End again before pressing the next arrow key. End mode is shown in the status bar when it is on.
	If the cells are blank, pressing End followed by an arrow key moves to the last cell in the row or column.
	End also selects the last command on the menu when a menu or submenu is visible.
	Ctrl+End moves to the last cell on a worksheet, to the lowest used row of the rightmost used column. If the cursor is in the formula bar, Ctrl+End moves the cursor to the end of the text.
	Ctrl+Shift+End extends the selection of cells to the last used cell on the worksheet (lower-right corner). If the cursor is in the formula bar, Ctrl+Shift+End selects all text in the

	formula bar from the cursor position to the end—this does not affect the height of the formula bar.
Enter	Completes a cell entry from the cell or the Formula Bar, and selects the cell below (by default). In a data form, it moves to the first field in the next record. Opens a selected menu (press F10 to activate the menu bar) or performs the action for a selected command. In a dialog box, it performs the action for the default command button in the dialog box (the button with the bold outline, often the **OK** button). Alt+Enter starts a new line in the same cell. Ctrl+Enter fills the selected cell range with the current entry. Shift+Enter completes a cell entry and selects the cell above.
Esc	Cancels an entry in the cell or Formula Bar. Closes an open menu or submenu, dialog box, or message window. It also closes full screen mode when this mode has been applied, and returns to

	normal screen mode to display the ribbon and status bar again.
Home	Moves to the beginning of a row in a worksheet. Moves to the cell in the upper-left corner of the window when Scroll Lock is turned on. Selects the first command on the menu when a menu or submenu is visible. Ctrl+Home moves to the beginning of a worksheet. Ctrl+Shift+Home extends the selection of cells to the beginning of the worksheet.
Page Down	Moves one screen down in a worksheet. Alt+Page Down moves one screen to the right in a worksheet. Ctrl+Page Down moves to the next sheet in a workbook. Ctrl+Shift+Page Down selects the current and next sheet in a workbook.
Page Up	Moves one screen up in a worksheet. Alt+Page Up moves one screen to the left in a worksheet. Ctrl+Page Up moves to the previous sheet in a workbook.

	Ctrl+Shift+Page Up selects the current and previous sheet in a workbook.
Spacebar	In a dialog box, performs the action for the selected button, or selects or clears a check box.
	Ctrl+Spacebar selects an entire column in a worksheet.
	Shift+Spacebar selects an entire row in a worksheet.
	Ctrl+Shift+Spacebar selects the entire worksheet.
	• If the worksheet contains data, Ctrl+Shift+Spacebar selects the current region. Pressing Ctrl+Shift+Spacebar a second time selects the current region and its summary rows. Pressing Ctrl+Shift+Spacebar a third time selects the entire worksheet. • When an object is selected, Ctrl+Shift+Spacebar selects all objects on a worksheet.
	Alt+Spacebar displays the **Control** menu for the Excel window.
Tab	Moves one cell to the right in a worksheet.
	Moves between unlocked cells in a protected worksheet.

| | Moves to the next option or option group in a dialog box.

Shift+Tab moves to the previous cell in a worksheet or the previous option in a dialog box.

Ctrl+Tab switches to the next tab in dialog box.

Ctrl+Shift+Tab switches to the previous tab in a dialog box. |
|---|---|

CHAPTER 7.

Keyboard Shortcuts In Outlook 2013.

Definition of Program: Microsoft Outlook is a program designed by Microsoft Corporation that keeps people connected through its email services with powerful organizational tools.

The following list of shortcut keys will help you to excel in Microsoft Outlook.

Basic Navigation

TASK	SHORTCUT
Switch to Mail.	Ctrl+1
Switch to Calendar.	Ctrl+2
Switch to Contacts.	Ctrl+3
Switch to Tasks.	Ctrl+4
Switch to Notes.	Ctrl+5
Switch to Folder List in Folder Pane.	Ctrl+6
Switch to Shortcuts.	Ctrl+7
Switch to next message (with message open).	Ctrl+Period
Switch to previous message (with message open).	Ctrl+Comma
Move between the Folder Pane, the main Outlook window, the Reading Pane, and the To-Do Bar.	Ctrl+Shift+Tab or Shift+Tab
Move between the Outlook window, the smaller panes in the	Tab

Folder Pane, the Reading Pane, and the sections in the To-Do Bar.	
Move between the Outlook window, the smaller panes in the Folder Pane, the Reading Pane, and the sections in the To-Do Bar, and show the access keys in the Outlook ribbon.	F6
Move around message header lines in the Folder Pane or an open message.	Ctrl+Tab
Move around within the Folder Pane.	Arrow keys
Go to a different folder.	Ctrl+Y
Go to the Search box.	F3 or Ctrl+E
In the Reading Pane, go to the previous message.	Alt+Up Arrow or Ctrl+Comma or Alt+Page Up
In the Reading Pane, page down through text.	Spacebar
In the Reading Pane, page up through text.	Shift+Spacebar
Collapse or expand a group in the email message list.	Left Arrow or Right Arrow, respectively
Go back to previous view in main Outlook window.	Alt+B or Alt+Left Arrow
Go forward to next view in main Outlook window.	Alt+Right Arrow
Select the InfoBar and, if available, show the menu of commands.	Ctrl+Shift+W

Search

TASK	SHORTCUT
Find a message or other item.	Ctrl+E

Clear the search results.	Esc
Expand the search to include **All Mail Items**, **All Calendar Items**, or **All Contact Items**, depending on the module you are in.	Ctrl+Alt+A
Use **Advanced Find**.	Ctrl+Shift+F
Create a Search Folder.	Ctrl+Shift+P
Search for text within an open item.	F4
Find and replace text, symbols, or some formatting commands. Works in the **Reading Pane** on an open item.	Ctrl+H
Expand search to include items from the current folder.	Ctrl+Alt+K
Expand search to include subfolders.	Ctrl+Alt+Z

Common Commands

Commands common to most views

TASK	SHORTCUT
Save (except in Tasks).	Ctrl+S or Shift+F12
Save and close (except in Mail).	Alt+S
Save as (only in Mail).	F12
Undo.	Ctrl+Z or Alt+Backspace
Delete an item.	Ctrl+D
Print.	Ctrl+P
Copy an item.	Ctrl+Shift+Y
Move an item.	Ctrl+Shift+V
Check names.	Ctrl+K
Check spelling.	F7
Flag for follow-up.	Ctrl+Shift+G
Forward.	Ctrl+F
Send or post or invite all.	Alt+S

Enable editing in a field (except in Mail or Icon view).	F2
Left align text.	Ctrl+L
Center text.	Ctrl+E
Right align text.	Ctrl+R

Format text

TASK	SHORTCUT
Display the **Format** menu.	Alt+O
Display the **Font** dialog box.	Ctrl+Shift+P
Switch case (with text selected).	Shift+F3
Format letters as small capitals.	Ctrl+Shift+K
Make letters bold.	Ctrl+B
Add bullets.	Ctrl+Shift+L
Make letters italic.	Ctrl+I
Increase indent.	Ctrl+T
Decrease indent.	Ctrl+Shift+T
Left align.	Ctrl+L
Center.	Ctrl+E
Underline.	Ctrl+U
Increase font size.	Ctrl+] or Ctrl+Shift+>
Decrease font size.	Ctrl+[or Ctrl+Shift+<
Cut.	Ctrl+X or Shift+Delete
Copy.	Ctrl+C or Ctrl+Insert **Note:** Ctrl+Insert is not available in the Reading Pane.
Paste.	Ctrl+V or Shift+Insert
Clear formatting.	Ctrl+Shift+Z or Ctrl+Spacebar
Delete the next word.	Ctrl+Shift+H

Stretch a paragraph to fit between the margins.	Ctrl+Shift+J
Apply styles.	Ctrl+Shift+S
Create a hanging indent.	Ctrl+T
Insert a hyperlink.	Ctrl+K
Left align a paragraph.	Ctrl+L
Right align a paragraph.	Ctrl+R
Reduce a hanging indent.	Ctrl+Shift+T
Remove paragraph formatting.	Ctrl+Q

Add links and edit URLs

TASK	SHORTCUT
Edit a URL in the body of an item.	Hold down Ctrl and click the mouse button.
Insert a hyperlink.	Ctrl+K

Create an item or file

TASK	SHORTCUT
Create an appointment.	Ctrl+Shift+A
Create a contact.	Ctrl+Shift+C
Create a contact group.	Ctrl+Shift+L
Create a fax.	Ctrl+Shift+X
Create a folder.	Ctrl+Shift+E
Create a meeting request.	Ctrl+Shift+Q
Create a message.	Ctrl+Shift+M
Create a note.	Ctrl+Shift+N
Create a Microsoft Office document.	Ctrl+Shift+H
Post to this folder.	Ctrl+Shift+S

Post a reply in this folder.	Ctrl+T
Create a Search Folder.	Ctrl+Shift+P
Create a task.	Ctrl+Shift+K
Create a task request.	Ctrl+Shift+U

Color Categories

TASK	SHORTCUT
Delete the selected category from the list in the Color Categories dialog box.	Alt+D

Flags

TASK	SHORTCUT
Open the **Flag for Follow Up** dialog box to assign a flag.	Ctrl+Shift+G

Mail

TASK	SHORTCUT
Switch to **Inbox**.	Ctrl+Shift+I
Switch to **Outbox**.	Ctrl+Shift+O
Choose the account from which to send a message.	Ctrl+Tab (with focus on the **To** box), and then Tab to the **Accounts** button
Check names.	Ctrl+K
Send.	Alt+S
Reply to a message.	Ctrl+R
Reply all to a message.	Ctrl+Shift+R
Reply with meeting request.	Ctrl+Alt+R
Forward a message.	Ctrl+F
Mark a message as not junk.	Ctrl+ Alt+J

Display blocked external content (in a message).	Ctrl+Shift+I
Post to a folder.	Ctrl+ Shift+S
Apply Normal style.	Ctrl+Shift+N
Check for new messages.	Ctrl+M or F9
Go to the previous message.	Up Arrow
Go to the next message.	Down Arrow
Create a message (when in Mail).	Ctrl+N
Create a message (from any Outlook view).	Ctrl+Shift+M
Open a received message.	Ctrl+O
Delete and Ignore a Conversation.	Ctrl+Shift+D
Open the Address Book.	Ctrl+Shift+B
Add a Quick Flag to an unopened message.	Insert
Display the **Flag for Follow Up** dialog box.	Ctrl+Shift+G
Mark as read.	Ctrl+Q
Mark as unread.	Ctrl+U
Open the Mail Tip in the selected message.	Ctrl+Shift+W
Find or replace.	F4
Find next.	Shift+F4
Send.	Ctrl+Enter
Print.	Ctrl+P
Forward.	Ctrl+F
Forward as attachment.	Ctrl+Alt+F
Show the properties for the selected item.	Alt+Enter

Create a multimedia message	Ctrl+Shift+U
Mark for Download.	Ctrl+Alt+M
Clear Mark for Download.	Ctrl+Alt+U
Display Send/Receive progress.	Ctrl+B (when a Send/Receive is in progress)

Calendar

TASK	SHORTCUT
Create an appointment (when in Calendar).	Ctrl+N
Create an appointment (in any Outlook view).	Ctrl+Shift+A
Create a meeting request.	Ctrl+Shift+Q
Forward an appointment or meeting.	Ctrl+F
Reply to a meeting request with a message.	Ctrl+R
Reply All to a meeting request with a message.	Ctrl+Shift+R
Show 1 day in the calendar.	Alt+1
Show 2 days in the calendar.	Alt+2
Show 3 days in the calendar.	Alt+3
Show 4 days in the calendar.	Alt+4
Show 5 days in the calendar.	Alt+5
Show 6 days in the calendar.	Alt+6
Show 7 days in the calendar.	Alt+7
Show 8 days in the calendar.	Alt+8
Show 9 days in the calendar.	Alt+9
Show 10 days in the calendar.	Alt+0
Go to a date.	Ctrl+G
Switch to Month view.	Alt+= or Ctrl+Alt+4
Go to the next day.	Ctrl+Right Arrow

Go to the next week.	Alt+Down Arrow
Go to the next month.	Alt+Page Down
Go to the previous day.	Ctrl+Left Arrow
Go to the previous week.	Alt+Up Arrow
Go to the previous month.	Alt+Page Up
Go to the start of the week.	Alt+Home
Go to the end of the week.	Alt+End
Switch to Full Week view.	Alt+Minus Sign or Ctrl+Alt+3
Switch to Work Week view.	Ctrl+Alt+2
Go to previous appointment.	Ctrl+Comma or Ctrl+Shift+Comma
Go to next appointment.	Ctrl+Period or Ctrl+Shift+Period
Set up recurrence for an open appointment or meeting.	Ctrl+G

See also under Views, Calendar Day/Week/Month view, and Date Navigator.

People

TASK	SHORTCUT
Dial a new call.	Ctrl+Shift+D
Find a contact or other item (Search).	F3 or Ctrl+E
Enter a name in the **Search Address Books** box.	F11
In Table or List view of contacts, go to first contact that starts with a specific letter.	Shift+letter
Select all contacts.	Ctrl+A
Create a message with selected contact as subject.	Ctrl+F
Create a contact (when in Contacts).	Ctrl+N

Create a contact (from any Outlook view).	Ctrl+Shift+C
Open a contact form for the selected contact.	Ctrl+O
Create a contact group.	Ctrl+Shift+L
Print.	Ctrl+P
Update a list of contact group members.	F5
Go to a different folder.	Ctrl+Y
Open the Address Book.	Ctrl+Shift+B
Use **Advanced Find**.	Ctrl+Shift+F
In an open contact, open the next contact listed.	Ctrl+Shift+Period
Find a contact.	F11
Close a contact.	ESC
Send a fax to the selected contact.	Ctrl+Shift+X
Open the **Check Address** dialog box.	Alt+D
In a contact form, under **Internet**, display the **Email 1** information.	Alt+Shift+1
In a contact form, under **Internet**, display the **Email 2** information.	Alt+Shift+2
In a contact form, under **Internet**, display the **Email 3** information.	Alt+Shift+3

Electronic Business Cards

TASK	SHORTCUT
Open the **Add** list.	Alt+A
Select text in **Label** box when the field with a label assigned is selected.	Alt+B
Open the **Add Card Picture** dialog box.	Alt+C
Place cursor at beginning of **Edit** box.	Alt+E
Select the **Fields** box.	Alt+F

Select the **Image Align** drop-down list.	Alt+G
Select color palette for background.	Alt+K, then Enter
Select **Layout** drop-down list.	Alt+L
Remove a selected field from the **Fields** box.	Alt+R

Tasks

TASK	SHORTCUT
Accept a task request.	Alt+C
Decline a task request.	Alt+D
Find a task or other item.	Ctrl+E
Open the **Go to Folder** dialog box.	Ctrl+Y
Create a task (when in Tasks).	Ctrl+N
Create a task (from any Outlook view).	Ctrl+Shift+K
Open selected item.	Ctrl+O
Print selected item.	Ctrl+P
Select all items.	Ctrl+A
Delete selected item.	Ctrl+D
Forward a task as an attachment.	Ctrl+F
Create a task request.	Ctrl+Shift+Alt+U
Switch between the **Folder Pane**, **Tasks** list, and **To-Do Bar**.	Tab or Shift+Tab
Undo last action.	Ctrl+Z
Flag an item or mark complete.	Insert

Groups

TASK	SHORTCUT
Expand a single selected group.	Right Arrow
Collapse a single selected group.	Left Arrow
Select the previous group.	Up Arrow

Select the next group.	Down Arrow
Select the first group.	Home
Select the last group.	End
Select the first item on screen in an expanded group or the first item off screen to the right.	Right Arrow

Print

TASK	SHORTCUT
Open **Print** tab in Backstage view.	Press Alt+F, and then press P
To print an item from an open window.	Alt+F, press P, and then press F and press 1
Open **Page Setup** from **Print Preview**.	Alt+S or Alt+U
To select a printer from **Print Preview**.	Alt+F, press P, and then press I
To **Define Print Styles**.	Alt+F, press P, and then press L
To open **Print Options**.	Alt+F, press P, and then press R

Send/Receive

TASK	SHORTCUT
Start a send/receive for all defined Send/Receive groups with **Include this group in Send/Receive (F9)** selected. This can include headers, full items, specified folders, items less than a specific size, or any combination that you define.	F9

Start a send/receive for the current folder, retrieving full items (header, item, and any attachments).	Shift+F9
Start a send/receive.	Ctrl+M
Define Send/Receive groups.	Ctrl+Alt+S

Macros

TASK	SHORTCUT
Play macro.	Alt+F8

Views

Table view

TASK	SHORTCUT
Open an item.	Enter
Select all items.	Ctrl+A
Go to the item at the bottom of the screen.	Page Down
Go to the item at the top of the screen.	Page Up
Extend or reduce the selected items by one item.	Shift+Up Arrow or Shift+Down Arrow, respectively
Go to the next or previous item without extending the selection.	Ctrl+Up Arrow or Ctrl+Down Arrow, respectively
Select or cancel selection of the active item.	Ctrl+Spacebar

Business Cards view or Address Cards view

TASK	SHORTCUT
Select a specific card in the list.	One or more letters of the name that the card is filed under or

	the name of the field that you are sorting by
Select the previous card.	Up Arrow
Select the next card.	Down Arrow
Select the first card in the list.	Home
Select the last card in the list.	End
Select the first card on the current page.	Page Up
Select the first card on the next page.	Page Down
Select the closest card in the next column.	Right Arrow
Select the closest card in the previous column.	Left Arrow
Select or cancel selection of the active card.	Ctrl+Spacebar
Extend the selection to the previous card and cancel selection of cards after the starting point.	Shift+Up Arrow
Extend the selection to the next card and cancel selection of cards before the starting point.	Shift+Down Arrow
Extend the selection to the previous card, regardless of the starting point.	Ctrl+Shift+Up Arrow

Extend the selection to the next card, regardless of the starting point.	Ctrl+Shift+Down Arrow
Extend the selection to the first card in the list.	Shift+Home
Extend the selection to the last card in the list.	Shift+End
Extend the selection to the first card on the previous page.	Shift+Page Up
Extend the selection to the last card on the last page.	Shift+Page Down

Move between fields in an open card

To use the following keys, make sure a field in a card is selected. To select a field when a card is selected, click the field.

TASK	SHORTCUT
Move to the next field and control.	Tab
Move to the previous field and control.	Shift+Tab
Close the active card.	Enter

Move between characters in a field

To use the following keys, make sure a field in a card is selected. To select a field when a card is selected, click the field.

TASK	SHORTCUT
Add a line in a multiline field.	Enter
Move to the beginning of a line.	Home
Move to the end of a line.	End

Move to the beginning of a multiline field.	Page Up
Move to the end of a multiline field.	Page Down
Move to the previous line in a multiline field.	Up Arrow
Move to the next line in a multiline field.	Down Arrow
Move to the previous character in a field.	Left Arrow
Move to the next character in a field.	Right Arrow

Timeline view (Tasks)

When an item is selected

TASK	SHORTCUT
Select the previous item.	Left Arrow
Select the next item.	Right Arrow
Select several adjacent items.	Shift+Left Arrow or Shift+Right Arrow
Select several nonadjacent items.	Ctrl+Left Arrow+Spacebar or Ctrl+Right Arrow+Spacebar
Open the selected items.	Enter
Select the first item on the timeline (if items are not grouped) or the first item in the group.	Home
Select the last item on the timeline (if items are not grouped) or the last item in the group.	End
Display (without selecting) the first item on the timeline (if items are not grouped) or the first item in the group.	Ctrl+Home

Display (without selecting) the last item on the timeline (if items are not grouped) or the last item in the group.	Ctrl+End

When a group is selected

TASK	SHORTCUT
Expand the group.	Enter or Right Arrow
Collapse the group.	Enter or Left Arrow
Select the previous group.	Up Arrow
Select the next group.	Down Arrow
Select the first group on the timeline.	Home
Select the last group on the timeline.	End
Select the first item on screen in an expanded group or the first item off screen to the right.	Right Arrow

When a unit of time on the time scale for days is selected.

TASK	SHORTCUT
Move back in increments of time that are the same as those shown on the time scale.	Left Arrow
Move forward in increments of time that are the same as those shown on the time scale.	Right Arrow
Switch between active view, To-Do Bar, Search and back to active view.	Tab and Shift+Tab

Calendar Day/Week/Month view

TASK	SHORTCUT
View from 1 through 9 days.	Alt+key for number of days

View 10 days.	Alt+0 (zero)
Switch to weeks.	Alt+Minus Sign
Switch to months.	Alt+=
Move between **Calendar**, **TaskPad**, and the **Folder List**.	Ctrl+Tab or F6
Select the previous appointment.	Shift+Tab
Go to the previous day.	Left Arrow
Go to the next day.	Right Arrow
Go to the same day in the next week.	Alt+Down Arrow
Go to the same day in the previous week.	Alt+Up Arrow

Day view

TASK	SHORTCUT
Select the time that begins your work day.	HOME
Select the time that ends your work day.	END
Select the previous block of time.	Up Arrow
Select the next block of time.	Down Arrow
Select the block of time at the top of the screen.	Page Up
Select the block of time at the bottom of the screen.	Page Down
Extend or reduce the selected time.	Shift+Up Arrow or Shift+Down Arrow, respectively
Move an appointment up or down.	With the cursor in the appointment, Alt+Up Arrow or Alt+Down Arrow, respectively

Change an appointment's start or end time.	With the cursor in the appointment, Alt+Shift+Up Arrow or Alt+Shift+Down Arrow, respectively
Move selected item to the same day in the next week.	Alt+Down Arrow
Move selected item to the same day in the previous week.	Alt+Up Arrow

Week view

TASK	SHORTCUT
Go to the start of work hours for the selected day.	Home
Go to the end of work hours for the selected day.	End
Go up one page view in the selected day.	Page Up
Go down one page view in the selected day.	Page Down
Change the duration of the selected block of time.	Shift+Left Arrow, Shift+Right Arrow, Shift+Up Arrow, or Shift+Down Arrow; or Shift+Home or Shift+End

Month view

TASK	SHORTCUT
Go to the first day of the week.	Home

Go to the same day of the week in the previous page.	Page Up
Go to the same day of the week in the next page.	Page Down

Date Navigator

TASK	SHORTCUT
Go to the first day of the current week.	Alt+Home
Go to the last day of the current week.	Alt+End
Go to the same day in the previous week.	Alt+Up Arrow
Go to the same day in the next week.	Alt+Down Arrow

CHAPTER 8.

Keyboard Shortcuts In OneNote 2013.

Definition of Program: Microsoft OneNote is a program designed by Microsoft Corporation in the year 2003 that is used for note-taking.

The following list of shortcut keys will help you to excel in Microsoft OneNote.

Taking And Formatting Notes

Typing and editing notes

TASK	SHORTCUT
Open a new OneNote window.	CTRL+M
Open a small OneNote window to create a side note.	CTRL+SHIFT+M or Windows+ALT+N
Dock the OneNote window.	CTRL+ALT+D
Undo the last action.	CTRL+Z
Redo the last action.	CTRL+Y
Select all items on the current page. **Note:** Press CTRL+A more than once to increase the scope of the selection.	CTRL+A
Cut the selected text or item.	CTRL+X
Copy the selected text or item to the Clipboard.	CTRL+C

Paste the contents of the Clipboard.	CTRL+V
Move to the beginning of the line.	HOME
Move to the end of the line.	END
Move one character to the left.	LEFT ARROW
Move one character to the right.	RIGHT ARROW
Move one word to the left.	CTRL+LEFT ARROW
Move one word to the right.	CTRL+RIGHT ARROW
Delete one character to the left.	BACKSPACE
Delete one character to the right.	DELETE
Delete one word to the left.	CTRL+BACKSPACE
Delete one word to the right.	CTRL+DELETE
Insert a line break without starting a new paragraph.	SHIFT+ENTER
Check spelling.	F7
Open the thesaurus for the currently selected word.	SHIFT+F7
Bring up the context menu for any note, tab, or any other object that currently has focus.	SHIFT+F10
Execute the action suggested on the Information Bar if it appears at the top of a page.	CTRL+SHIFT+W

Formatting notes

TASK	SHORTCUT
Highlight selected text.	CTRL+SHIFT+H or CTRL+ALT+H

Insert a link.	CTRL+K
Copy the formatting of selected text (Format Painter).	CTRL+SHIFT+C
Paste the formatting to selected text (Format Painter).	CTRL+SHIFT+V
Open a link. **Note:** The cursor must be placed anywhere within the formatted link text.	ENTER
Apply or remove bold formatting from the selected text.	CTRL+B
Apply or remove italic formatting from the selected text.	CTRL+I
Apply or remove the underline from the selected text.	CTRL+U
Apply or remove strikethrough from the selected text.	CTRL+HYPHEN
Apply or remove superscript formatting from the selected text.	CTRL+SHIFT+=
Apply or remove subscript formatting from the selected text.	CTRL+=
Apply or remove bulleted list formatting from the selected paragraph.	CTRL+PERIOD

Apply or remove numbered list formatting from the selected paragraph.	CTRL+SLASH
Apply a Heading 1 style to the current note.	CTRL+ALT+1
Apply a Heading 2 style to the current note.	CTRL+ALT+2
Apply a Heading 3 style to the current note.	CTRL+ALT+3
Apply a Heading 4 style to the current note.	CTRL+ALT+4
Apply a Heading 5 style to the current note.	CTRL+ALT+5
Apply a Heading 6 style to the current note.	CTRL+ALT+6
Apply the Normal style to the current note.	CTRL+SHIFT+N
Indent a paragraph from the left.	ALT+SHIFT+RIGHT ARROW
Remove a paragraph indent from the left.	ALT+SHIFT+LEFT ARROW
Right-align the selected paragraph.	CTRL+R
Left-align the selected paragraph.	CTRL+L
Increase the font size of selected text.	CTRL+SHIFT+>
Decrease the font size of selected text.	CTRL+SHIFT+<
Clear all formatting applied to the selected text.	CTRL+SHIFT+N
Show or hide rule lines on the current page.	CTRL+SHIFT+R

Adding items to a page

TASK	SHORTCUT
Insert a document or file on the current page.	ALT+N, F
Insert a document or file as a printout on the current page.	ALT+N, O
Show or hide document printouts on the current page (when running OneNote in High Contrast mode).	ALT+SHIFT+P
Insert a picture from a file.	ALT+N, P
Insert a picture from a scanner or a camera.	ALT+N, S
Insert a screen clipping. **Note:** The OneNote icon must be active in the notification area, at the far right of the Windows taskbar.	Windows logo key+S (If you're using OneNote 2013 with the latest updates, press Windows logo key+SHIFT+S)
Insert the current date.	ALT+SHIFT+D
Insert the current date and time.	ALT+SHIFT+F
Insert the current time.	ALT+SHIFT+T
Insert a line break.	SHIFT+ENTER
Start a math equation or convert selected text to a math equation.	ALT+=
Insert a Euro (€) symbol.	CTRL+ALT+E

Create a table by adding a second column to already typed text.	TAB
Create another column in a table with a single row.	TAB
Create another row when at the end cell of a table. **Note:** Press ENTER a second time to finish the table.	ENTER
Create a row below the current row in a table.	CTRL+ENTER
Create another paragraph in the same cell in a table.	ALT+ENTER
Create a column to the right of the current column in a table.	CTRL+ALT+R
Create a row above the current one in a table (when the cursor is at the beginning of any row).	ENTER
Delete the current empty row in a table (when the cursor is at the beginning of the row).	DEL (press twice)

Selecting notes and objects

TASK	SHORTCUT
Select all items on the current page.	CTRL+A

Note: Press CTRL+A more than once to increase the scope of the selection.	
Select to the end of the line.	SHIFT+END
Select the whole line (when the cursor is at the beginning of the line).	SHIFT+DOWN ARROW
Jump to the title of the page and select it.	CTRL+SHIFT+T
Cancel the selected outline or page.	ESC
Move the current paragraph or several selected paragraphs up.	ALT+SHIFT+UP ARROW
Move the current paragraph or several selected paragraphs down.	ALT+SHIFT+DOWN ARROW
Move the current paragraph or several selected paragraphs left (decreasing the indent).	ALT+SHIFT+LEFT ARROW
Move the current paragraph or several selected paragraphs right (increasing the indent).	ALT+SHIFT+RIGHT ARROW
Select the current paragraph and its subordinate paragraphs.	CTRL+SHIFT+HYPHEN
Delete the selected note or object.	DELETE
Move to the beginning of the line.	HOME
Move to the end of the line.	END
Move one character to the left.	LEFT ARROW

Move one character to the right.	RIGHT ARROW
Go back to the last page visited.	ALT+LEFT ARROW
Go forward to the next page visited.	ALT+RIGHT ARROW
Start playback of a selected audio or video recording.	CTRL+ALT+P or CTRL+ALT+S
Rewind the current audio or video recording by a few seconds.	CTRL+ALT+Y
Fast-forward the current audio or video recording by a few seconds.	CTRL+ALT+U

Tagging notes

TASK	SHORTCUT
Apply, mark, or clear the To Do tag.	CTRL+1
Apply or clear the Important tag.	CTRL+2
Apply or clear the Question tag.	CTRL+3
Apply or clear the Remember for later tag.	CTRL+4
Apply or clear the Definition tag.	CTRL+5
Apply or clear a custom tag.	CTRL+6
Apply or clear a custom tag.	CTRL+7
Apply or clear a custom tag.	CTRL+8
Apply or clear a custom tag.	CTRL+9
Remove all note tags from the selected notes.	CTRL+0

Using outlines

TASK	SHORTCUT
Show through Level 1.	ALT+SHIFT+1

Expand to Level 2.	ALT+SHIFT+2
Expand to Level 3.	ALT+SHIFT+3
Expand to Level 4.	ALT+SHIFT+4
Expand to Level 5.	ALT+SHIFT+5
Expand to Level 6.	ALT+SHIFT+6
Expand to Level 7.	ALT+SHIFT+7
Expand to Level 8.	ALT+SHIFT+8
Expand to Level 9.	ALT+SHIFT+9
Expand all levels.	ALT+SHIFT+0
Increase indent by one level.	TAB
Decrease indent by one level.	SHIFT+TAB
Expand a collapsed outline.	ALT+SHIFT+PLUS SIGN
Collapse an expanded outline.	ALT+SHIFT+MINUS SIGN

Specifying language settings

Note: To change the writing direction for your notes, you must first enable right-to-left languages in the **Microsoft Office Language Preferences** tool.

TASK	SHORTCUT
Set writing direction left to right.	CTRL+LEFT SHIFT
Set writing direction right to left.	CTRL+RIGHT SHIFT
Increase indent by one level in right-to-left text.	TAB
Decrease indent by one level in right-to-left text.	SHIFT+TAB

Organizing And Managing Your Notebook

Working with pages and side notes

TASK	SHORTCUT
Enable or disable full page view.	F11
Open a new OneNote window.	CTRL+M
Open a small OneNote window to create a side note.	CTRL+SHIFT+M
Expand or collapse the tabs of a page group.	CTRL+SHIFT+*
Print the current page.	CTRL+P
Add a new page at the end of the selected section.	CTRL+N
Increase the width of the page tabs bar.	CTRL+SHIFT+[
Decrease the width of the page tabs bar.	CTRL+SHIFT+]
Create a new page below the current page tab at the same level.	CTRL+ALT+N
Decrease indent level of the current page tab label.	CTRL+ALT+[
Increase indent level of the current page tab label.	CTRL+ALT+]
Create a new subpage below the current page.	CTRL+SHIFT+ALT+N

Select all items. **Note:** Press CTRL+A several times to increase the scope of the selection.	CTRL+A
Select the current page.	CTRL+SHIFT+A If the selected page is part of a group, press CTRL+A to select all of the pages in the group.
Move the selected page tab up.	ALT+SHIFT+UP ARROW
Move the selected page tab down.	ALT+SHIFT+DOWN ARROW
Move the insertion point to the page title.	CTRL+SHIFT+T
Go to the first page in the currently visible set of page tabs.	ALT+PAGE UP
Go to the last page in the currently visible set of page tabs.	ALT+PAGE DOWN
Scroll up in the current page.	PAGE UP
Scroll down in the current page.	PAGE DOWN
Scroll to the top of the current page.	CTRL+HOME
Scroll to the bottom of the current page.	CTRL+END

Go to the next paragraph.	CTRL+DOWN ARROW
Go to the previous paragraph.	CTRL+UP ARROW
Go to the next note container.	ALT+DOWN ARROW
Go to the beginning of the line.	HOME
Go to the end of the line.	END
Move one character to the left.	LEFT ARROW
Move one character to the right.	RIGHT ARROW
Go back to the last page visited.	ALT+LEFT ARROW
Go forward to the next page visited.	ALT+RIGHT ARROW
Zoom in.	ALT+CTRL+PLUS SIGN (on the numeric keypad) or ALT+CTRL+SHIFT+PLUS SIGN
Zoom out.	ALT+CTRL+MINUS SIGN (on the numeric keypad) or ALT+CTRL+SHIFT+HYPHEN
Save changes. **Note:** While OneNote is running, your notes are automatically saved whenever you change them. Manually saving notes is not necessary.	CTRL+S

Working with notebooks and sections

TASK	SHORTCUT
Open OneNote.	Windows+SHIFT+N
Open a notebook.	CTRL+O
Send to OneNote Tool	Windows+N
Create a new section.	CTRL+T
Open a section.	CTRL+ALT+SHIFT+O
Go to the next section.	CTRL+TAB
Go to the previous section.	CTRL+SHIFT+TAB
Go to the next page in the section.	CTRL+PAGE DOWN
Go to the previous page in the section.	CTRL+PAGE UP
Go to the first page in the section.	ALT+HOME
Go to the last page in the section.	ALT+END
Go to the first page in the currently visible set of page tabs.	ALT+PAGE UP
Go to the last page of the currently visible set of page tabs.	ALT+PAGE DOWN
Move or copy the current page.	CTRL+ALT+M

Put focus on the current page tab.	CTRL+ALT+G
Select the current page tab.	CTRL+SHFT+A
Put focus on the current section tab.	CTRL+SHIFT+G
Move the current section.	CTRL+SHIFT+G, and then SHIFT+F10, M
Switch to a different notebook on the Navigation bar.	CTRL+G, then press DOWN ARROW or UP ARROW keys to select a different notebook, and then press ENTER

Searching notes

TASK	SHORTCUT
Move the insertion point to the **Search** box to search all notebooks.	CTRL+E
While searching all notebooks, preview the next result.	DOWN ARROW
While searching all notebooks, go to the selected result and dismiss Search.	ENTER
Change the search scope.	CTRL+E, TAB, SPACE
Open the Search Results pane.	ALT+O after searching
Search only the current page. **Note:** You can switch between searching everywhere and searching only the current page at any point by pressing CRTL+E or CTRL+F.	CTRL+F
While searching the current page, move to the next result.	ENTER or F3

| While searching the current page, move to the previous result. | SHFT+F3 |
| Dismiss Search and return to the page. | ESC |

Sharing Notes.

Sharing notes with other people

TASK	SHORTCUT
Send the selected pages in an e-mail message.	CTRL+SHIFT+E

Sharing notes with other programs

TASK	SHORTCUT
Send the selected pages in an e-mail message.	CTRL+SHIFT+E
Create a **Today** Outlook task from the currently selected note.	CTRL+SHIFT+1
Create a **Tomorrow** Outlook task from the currently selected note.	CTRL+SHIFT+2
Create a **This Week** Outlook task from the currently selected note.	CTRL+SHIFT+3
Create a **Next Week** Outlook task from the currently selected note.	CTRL+SHIFT+4
Create a **No Date** Outlook task from the currently selected note.	CTRL+SHIFT+5
Open the selected Outlook task.	CTRL+SHIFT+K
Mark the selected Outlook task as complete.	CTRL+SHIFT+9
Delete the selected Outlook task.	CTRL+SHIFT+0
Sync changes in the current shared notebook.	SHIFT+F9
Sync changes in all shared notebooks.	F9
Mark the current page as Unread.	CTRL+Q

Protecting Notes.

Password-protecting sections

TASK	SHORTCUT
Lock all password-protected sections.	CTRL+ALT+L

Chapter 9.

Keyboard Shortcuts in Lync 2013.

Definition of Program: Lync is an instant messaging client that allows you to connect with your friends, family, coworkers, and many others cost-effectively.

The following list of shortcut keys will help you to excel in Microsoft Lync.

Tab and **Shift+Tab** are common ways of moving through any UI. **Tab** moves through the UI in order, whereas **Shift+Tab** moves through it in reverse order.

General (Any Window)

SHORTCUT	TASK
Windows logo key+Shift+O	Accept an incoming invite notification.
Windows logo key+Esc	Decline an invite notification.
Windows logo key+F4	Self-mute/unmute audio.
Windows logo key+F5	Turn my Camera On/Turn my Camera Off when video is already established in the call.
Ctrl+Shift+Spacebar	Put focus on the application sharing toolbar.
Ctrl+Alt+Shift+3	Open the main window and put focus in the search box.
Ctrl+Alt+Spacebar	Take back control when sharing your screen.

Ctrl+Shift+S	Stop sharing your screen.

Skype For Business Main Window

Use these keyboard shortcuts when the Skype for Business (Lync) main window is in the foreground.

SHORTCUT	TASK
Ctrl+1	Move to the Contacts list tab.
Ctrl+2	Move to the persistent chat tab.
Ctrl+3	Move to the Conversation list tab.
Ctrl+4	Move to the Phone tab.
Ctrl+1 or Ctrl+Shift+1	As a delegate, transfer a call to someone else's work number. (Not available in Lync Basic or with all Office 365 subscriptions.)
Alt+Spacebar	Open the System menu. Alt opens the menu bar.
Alt+F	Open the File menu.
Alt+M	Start Meet Now.
Alt+T	Open the Tools menu.
Alt+H	Open the Help menu.

Contacts List

Use these keyboard shortcuts while in the Contacts list.

SHORTCUT	TASK
Delete	Delete the selected custom group or contact.
Alt+Up Arrow	Move the selected group up.
Alt+Down Arrow	Move the selected group down.

Alt+Enter	On the shortcuts menu—open the selected contact or group contacts card.
Spacebar	Collapse or expand the selected group.
Shift+Delete	Remove the selected contact from the Contacts list (non-distribution-group members only).

Contact Card

Use these keyboard shortcuts while in a contact card. Use **Alt+Enter** to open a contact card.

SHORTCUT	TASK
Esc	Close the contact card.
Ctrl+Tab	Move through the tabs at the bottom of the contact card.
Ctrl+Shift+Tab	Move through the tabs at the bottom of the contact card in reverse order.

Conversation Window

Use these keyboard shortcuts while in the Conversation window.

SHORTCUT	TASK
F1	Open the Help home page (on the Help menu).
Esc	Exit full-screen view if present. Otherwise, the Conversation window closes only if there is no audio, video, or sharing occurring.
Alt+C	Accept any of the invite notifications. These include

	audio, video, call, and sharing requests.
Alt+F4	Close the Conversation window.
Alt+1	Ignore any invite notifications. These include audio, video, call, and sharing requests.
Alt+R	Rejoin audio in a meeting.
Alt+S	Open the **Save As** dialog box for a file that was sent in the Conversation window.
Alt+V	Invite a contact to an existing conversation.
Ctrl+S	Save the contents of IM history. Works for person-to-person conversations when you use Outlook.
Ctrl+W	Show or hide the instant message area.
Ctrl+F	Send a file, or in the context of a conference, add a meeting attachment.
Ctrl+N	Take your own notes by using Microsoft OneNote note-taking program. Starts OneNote. (Not available in Lync Basic.)
Ctrl+R	Show or hide the participant list.
Ctrl+Shift+Alt+Right Arrow	Navigate right to the next UI element in the Conversation window. This key combination replaces the Tab key for moving the focus from one UI element to the next.
Ctrl+Shift+Alt+Left Arrow	Navigate left to the previous UI element in the Conversation

	window. This key combination replaces the Tab key for moving the focus from one UI element to the previous one.
Ctrl+Shift+Enter	Add video/end video.
Ctrl+Shift+H	Hold or resume an ongoing audio conversation.
Ctrl+Shift+I	Mark a conversation as having high importance. Works for person-to-person conversations, but isn't available for meetings.
Ctrl+Shift+Y	Show or hide the sharing stage.
Ctrl+Shift+P	Switch to compact view.
Ctrl+Shift+K	Switch to content-only view.
Ctrl+Enter	Add audio/end audio.
Up Arrow	When on a mode button, opens the corresponding callout.
Spacebar	When focus is on a mode button, a default action is taken. So for audio, mute or unmute occurs, whereas for video, it starts or stops the camera.
Esc	Dismiss or hide an open callout or bubble that has keyboard focus.

Call Controls (Conversation Window)

Use these keyboard shortcuts in the call controls while in a peer-to-peer call. This doesn't work in a conference call.

SHORTCUT	TASK
Alt+Q	End a call.

Ctrl+Shift+T	Transfer: Open the contact picker during a peer-to-peer call. (Not available in Lync Basic or with all Office 365 subscriptions.)
Ctrl+Shift+H	Put a call on hold.
Ctrl+Shift+D	Display the dial pad.

Video (Conversation Window)

Use these keyboard shortcuts when you're working with video in the Conversation window.

SHORTCUT	TASK
F5	View video in full screen. If the stage area is visible in the Conversation window, F5 won't take full-screen video.
Esc	Exit full-screen video.
Ctrl+Shift+O	Pop out Gallery; Pop in Gallery.
Ctrl+Shift+L	Lock your video for everyone in the meeting.

IM (Conversation Window)

Use these keyboard shortcuts when you're in an IM with someone.

SHORTCUT	TASK
F1	Open Help.
F12	Save the IM conversation.
Shift+Enter	Add carriage returns.
Shift+Insert or Ctrl+V	Paste.
Ctrl+A	Select all content.
Ctrl+B	Make the selected text bold.
Ctrl+C	Copy the selected text.

Ctrl+X	Cut the selected text.
Ctrl+I	Italicize the selected text.
Ctrl+U	Underline the selected text.
Ctrl+Y	Redo the last action.
Ctrl+Z	Undo the last action.
Ctrl+Shift+F	Change the color of the font. (Only changes color for what you type, not for what the other person types.)
Alt+P	Open a file that's been received.
Alt+D	Decline a file that's been sent.
Ctrl+Shift+M	To get focus to your IM input area.

Conversation or Meeting Stage

SHORTCUT	TASK
F5	View the Conversation window meeting stage in full screen.
Esc	Exit full screen if present.
Alt+T	Stop sharing.
Ctrl+Shift+E	Manage presentable content.
Ctrl+Shift+Y	Show or hide the sharing stage.
Ctrl+Shift+A	Force pending L1 alert into view in full screen.
Ctrl+Shift+J	Switch to speaker view.
Ctrl+Shift+I	Switch to gallery view.
Ctrl+Alt+Right Arrow or

Ctrl+Alt+Left Arrow | Tab out of the sharing region in a forward direction, and/or tab out of the sharing region in a backward direction. |

Conversation Environment

SHORTCUT	TASK
Delete	Delete selected items.

Home	Move top of list.
End	Move to bottom of list.
Page Up	Move one page up.
Page Down	Move one page down.
Up Arrow	Move up to the previous contact for conversation.
Down Arrow	Move down to the next contact for conversation.

PPT Sharing: Legacy PPT Viewer

SHORTCUT	TASK
Tab	When the content space is in focus, tab through the controls for PPT sharing (Prev arrow, Next arrow, Thumbnails, and Notes).
Right Arrow	When focus is on content area, move to the next click, or slide, if no click for animation is on the current slide.
Left or Right Arrow	When the thumbnail area is in focus, move focus to the previous or next thumbnail without changing the active slide.
Left Arrow	When focus is on content area, move to the previous click, or slide if no click for animation is on the current slide.
Home	When thumbnail area is in focus, set the focus on the first slide thumbnail without changing the active slide.
Enter	Select the control in focus or thumbnails if thumbnail strip has focus and select (change in active slide).
End	When the thumbnail area is in focus, set the focus on the last slide

	thumbnail without changing the active slide.

Tabbed Conversations

SHORTCUT	TASK
Alt+Spacebar	Open tab window's system menu.
Ctrl+Shift+T	Set focus on tab item in tabbed conversation view.
Ctrl+Tab	Switch to the next tab (continuously loop through all tabs).
Ctrl+1,2...9	Switch to a specific tab number and put keyboard focus in that conversation. Ctrl+1.
Ctrl+O	Undock/dock the selected conversation from/to the tab window.
Esc	Close a tab.

CHAPTER 10.

Keyboard Shortcuts In InfoPath 2013.

Definition of Program: Microsoft InfoPath is an electronic Program used to design, fill and submit electronic forms that has to do with structured data. It is a Microsoft Corporation program first released in 2003.

The following list of shortcut keys will help you to excel in Microsoft InfoPath.

Fill Out An InfoPath Form

Fill out forms in InfoPath

TASK	SHORTCUT
Navigate to next control in tab order.	Tab
Navigate to previous control in tab order.	SHIFT+TAB
Navigate to control above.	ALT+UP
Navigate to control below.	ALT+DOWN
Date Picker control: display the calendar.	Down arrow
Navigate to next field that has an error.	CTRL+SHIFT+O
Get error details for current field if it contains an error.	CTRL+SHIFT+I
Expose the widget menu for a control that supports it.	ALT+SHIFT+F10

Repeating table/repeating section: Add a row or section while inside the control.	CTRL+ENTER

Format text in a rich text control

TASK	SHORTCUT
Remove all formatting.	CTRL+SPACEBAR
Apply or remove bold formatting from the selected text.	CTRL+B
Apply or remove italic formatting from the selected text.	CTRL+I
Apply or remove the underline from the selected text.	CTRL+U
Apply or remove strikethrough from the selected text.	ALT+SHIFT+K
Apply or remove superscript formatting from the selected text.	CTRL+SHIFT+EQUAL SIGN
Apply or remove subscript formatting from the selected text.	CTRL+EQUAL SIGN
Apply the Normal style to the selected text.	CTRL+SHIFT+N
Apply the Title style from the selected text.	ALT+CTRL+1
Apply the Heading 1 style from the selected text	ALT+CTRL+2
Apply the Heading 2 style from the selected text.	ALT+CTRL+3

Apply the label style from the selected text.	ALT+CTRL+4
Apply the column label style from the selected text.	ALT+CTRL+5
Apply the description style from the selected text.	ALT+CTRL+6
Apply or remove bulleted list formatting from the selected paragraph.	CTRL+SHIFT+L
Indent a paragraph from the left.	CTRL+M
Remove a paragraph indent from the left.	CTRL+SHIFT+M
Justify the selected paragraph.	CTRL+J
Right align the selected paragraph.	CTRL+R
Center the selected paragraph.	CTRL+E
Left align the selected paragraph.	CTRL+L
Increase the font size for the selected text.	CTRL+SHIFT+COMMA
Decrease the font size for the selected text.	CTRL+SHIFT+PERIOD
Increase the font size for the selected text by 1 point.	CTRL+[
Decrease the font size for the selected text by 1 point.	CTRL+]
Open the **Font** task pane.	CTRL+SHIFT+F, CTRL+SHIFT+P, CTRL+D

Switch paragraph to right-to-left text direction.	CTRL+RIGHT SHIFT
Switch paragraph to left-to-right text direction.	CTRL+LEFT SHIFT

Fill out an InfoPath form in a web browser

TASK	SHORTCUT
Add a section to a repeating section control.	CTRL+ENTER
Remove a section from a repeating section control.	CTRL+DEL
Add a row to a repeating table control	CTRL+ENTER
Remove a row from a repeating table control.	CTRL+DEL
Navigate through fields that have errors in the current form view.	CTRL+SHIFT+O
Get error information for a field that has an error.	CTRL+SHIFT+I
Move focus to web ribbon tabs.	CTRL+[
Select tab in web ribbon.	Enter
Move focus to last-used web ribbon button.	CTRL+]
Return focus to page from the web ribbon.	Esc
Next rich text command (moves the focus to rich text toolbar from rich text box).	CTRL+1
Next rich text command (moves the focus to rich text toolbar from rich text box).	CTRL+'
Cut to Windows clipboard.	CTRL+X
Copy to Windows clipboard.	CTRL+C

Paste Windows clipboard.	CTRL+V
Clear format.	CTRL+SPACE
Undo last action.	CTRL+Z
Redo last action.	CTRL+Y
Open a new window to insert a table.	CTRL+ALT+T
Split cells.	CTRL+ALT+S
Merge cells.	CTRL+ALT+M
Open a new window to insert a hyperlink.	CTRL+K
Open a new window to insert a picture.	CTRL+SHIFT+G
Select font.	CTRL+SHIFT+F
Change font size.	CTRL+SHIFT+P
Make text bold.	CTRL+B
Make text italic.	CTRL+I
Underline text.	CTRL+U
Align text left.	CTRL+L
Align text right.	CTRL+R
Align text centered.	CTRL+E
Insert number list.	CTRL+SHIFT+E
Insert bullet list.	CTRL+SHIFT+L
Decrease indent.	CTRL+SHIFT+M
Increase indent.	CTRL+M
Change text color.	CTRL+SHIFT+C
Highlight text.	CTRL+SHIFT+W
Switch text direction left-to-right.	CTRL+SHIFT+>
Switch text direction right-to-left.	CTRL+SHIFT+<

Design A Form In InfoPath Designer

TASK	SHORTCUT
Design a new form template.	CTRL+SHIFT+D
Open the **Open in design**	CTRL+O or CTRL+F12

mode dialog box.	
Display the **Design Tasks** task pane.	ALT+N **Note:** If the **Getting Started** dialog box is open, press the TAB key until you can select **Design a Form Template**. Then, press ENTER.
Preview the current form template.	CTRL+SHIFT+B
Find a word or phrase.	CTRL+F
Replace a word or phrase.	CTRL+H
Cut the selected text or item.	CTRL+X
Copy the selected text or item.	CTRL+C
Paste text or an item.	CTRL+V
Print the current form template.	CTRL+P
Display the properties of the selected control.	ALT+ENTER
Select the previous control.	CTRL+< (less than sign) or SHIFT+TAB
Select the next control.	CTRL+> (greater than sign) or TAB
Insert a hyperlink.	CTRL+K
Select to the beginning of the paragraph.	CTRL+SHIFT+UP ARROW

Select to the end of the paragraph.	CTRL+SHIFT+DOWN ARROW
Select the text, graphic, or field to one line up or one line down.	SHIFT+UP ARROW or SHIFT+DOWN ARROW
Insert a line break.	SHIFT+ENTER
Insert the euro symbol.	CTRL+ALT+E

Format text in a form template

TASK	SHORTCUT
Remove all formatting.	CTRL+SPACEBAR
Apply or remove bold formatting from the selected text.	CTRL+B
Apply or remove italic formatting from the selected text.	CTRL+I
Apply or remove the underline from the selected text.	CTRL+U
Apply or remove strikethrough from the selected text.	ALT+SHIFT+K
Apply or remove superscript formatting from the selected text.	CTRL+SHIFT+EQUAL SIGN
Apply or remove subscript formatting from the selected text.	CTRL+EQUAL SIGN
Apply the Normal style from the selected text.	CTRL+SHIFT+N

Apply the Title style from the selected text.	ALT+CTRL+1
Apply the Heading 1 style from the selected text	ALT+CTRL+2
Apply the Heading 2 style from the selected text.	ALT+CTRL+3
Apply the label style from the selected text.	ALT+CTRL+4
Apply column label style from the selected text.	ALT+CTRL+5
Apply the description style from the selected text.	ALT+CTRL+6
Apply or remove bulleted list formatting from the selected paragraph.	CTRL+SHIFT+L
Indent a paragraph from the left.	CTRL+M
Remove a paragraph indent from the left.	CTRL+SHIFT+M
Justify the selected paragraph.	CTRL+J
Right align the selected paragraph.	CTRL+R
Center the selected paragraph.	CTRL+E
Left align the selected paragraph.	CTRL+L
Increase the font size for the selected text.	CTRL+SHIFT+COMMA
Decrease the font size for the selected text.	CTRL+SHIFT+PERIOD
Increase the font size for the selected text by 1 point.	CTRL+[

Decrease the font size for the selected text by 1 point.	CTRL+]
Open the **Font** task pane.	CTRL+SHIFT+F, CTRL+SHIFT+P, CTRL+D
Switch paragraph to right-to-left text direction.	CTRL+RIGHT SHIFT
Switch paragraph to left-to-right text direction.	CTRL+LEFT SHIFT

Work with layout tables

TASK	SHORTCUT
Change the width of the column to the left of the border without changing the width of the other columns.	Hold down SHIFT while dragging the border of the column.
Change the height of the row above or below the border without changing the height of the other rows.	Hold down SHIFT while dragging the border of the row. **Note:** For rows that are sized at their minimum height, this shortcut changes the height of the row above the border. A row's minimum height is determined by several factors, such as whether it contains text or controls.
Resize all of the selected rows or columns to the same height or width.	Hold down ALT while dragging the border of the row or column.

Move between the next or previous cell in a table.	TAB or SHIFT+TAB TAB adds a new row to a table if you press it while the pointer is in the last cell of the last row.
Select or cancel the selection of a table cell.	F2

Make corrections and save changes

TASK	SHORTCUT
Find the next misspelling or grammatical error.	ALT+F7 **Note:** The **Check spelling as you type** check box must be selected (Press ALT+T, and then press **OK**).
Save or publish the current form template.	ALT+SHIFT+F2 **Note:** This shortcut opens a dialog box that offers a choice between saving and publishing your form template. If you choose to hide this dialog box in the future, pressing ALT+SHIFT+F2 displays the **Save As** dialog box.
Undo the last action.	CTRL+Z
Redo the last action.	CTRL+Y
Save the current form template.	CTRL+S
Open the **Save As** dialog box for the current form template.	SHIFT+F12 or ALT+SHIFT+F2

Print preview of form template

TASK	SHORTCUT
Display the **Print Preview** dialog box.	ALT+F, V
Move to the next page.	ALT+RIGHT ARROW
Move to the previous page.	ALT+LEFT ARROW
Zoom in to get a close-up view of the form template.	ALT+EQUAL SIGN
Zoom out to see more of the form template at a reduced size.	ALT+HYPHEN

Get Help

The Help window provides access to all Microsoft Office Help content. The Help window displays topics and other Help content.

TASK	SHORTCUT
Open the Help window.	F1 **Note:** If the current Help topic is not in the active window, press F6 and then press CTRL+P.
Close the Help window.	ALT+F4
Switch between the Help window and the active program.	ALT+TAB
Select the next item.	TAB
Select the previous item.	SHIFT+TAB
Perform the default action for the selected item.	ENTER

In the **Browse Program Name Help** section, select the next or previous item.	TAB or SHIFT+TAB
In the **Browse Program Name Help** section, expand or collapse the selected item.	ENTER
Select the next hidden text or hyperlink, such as **Show All** or **Hide All** at the top of a topic.	TAB
Select the previous hidden text or hyperlink.	SHIFT+TAB
Perform the action for the selected **Show All**, **Hide All**, hidden text, or hyperlink.	ENTER
Move back to the previous Help topic (**Back** button).	ALT+LEFT ARROW or BACKSPACE
Move forward to the next Help topic (**Forward** button).	ALT+RIGHT ARROW
Scroll small amounts up or down within the currently displayed Help topic.	UP ARROW, DOWN ARROW
Scroll larger amounts up or down within the currently displayed Help topic.	PAGE UP, PAGE DOWN
Display a menu of commands for the Help window. This requires that the Help window have the active focus (press F1).	SHIFT+F10
Stop the last action (**Stop** button).	ESC

Refresh the window (**Refresh** button).	F5
Print the current Help topic.	CTRL+P
Change the connection state.	F6, DOWN ARROW
Switch among areas in the Help window. For example, switch between the toolbar, the search box, and the help connections status.	F6
In the table of contents in tree view, select the next or previous item.	UP ARROW or DOWN ARROW
In the table of contents in tree view, expand or collapse the selected item.	LEFT ARROW or RIGHT ARROW
Select the next hyperlink, or select **Show All** or **Hide All** at the top of a topic.	TAB
Select the previous hyperlink.	SHIFT+TAB
Perform the action for the selected hyperlink, **Show All**, or **Hide All**.	ENTER
Print the current Help topic.	CTRL+P

Use dialog boxes

Access and select options in dialog boxes

TASK	SHORTCUT
Open the **Open in design mode** dialog box.	CTRL+O or CTRL+F12
Move from an open dialog box back to the	ALT+F6

form template, for dialog boxes that support this behavior.	
Move to the next option.	TAB
Move to the previous option.	SHIFT+TAB
Switch to the next tab.	CTRL+TAB
Switch to the previous tab.	CTRL+SHIFT+TAB
Switch to the next category.	TAB **Note:** After the category is selected, use the arrow keys to move to the category name that you want.
Switch to the previous category.	SHIFT+TAB **Note:** After the category is selected, use the arrow keys to move to the category that you want.
Move between options in a list or group of options.	Arrow keys
Perform the action assigned to the selected button, or select or clear the selected check box.	SPACEBAR
Open the list if it is closed and move to a specific option in the list.	First letter of an option in a drop-down list
Select an option, or select or clear a check box.	ALT+ the letter underlined in an option
Open the selected drop-down list.	DOWN ARROW

Close the selected drop-down list, or cancel a command and then close the dialog box.	ESC
Run the selected command.	ENTER
Go to the previous folder.	ALT+1
Open the folder one level up from the selected folder.	ALT+2
Delete the selected folder or file.	ALT+3
Create a subfolder in the open folder.	ALT+4
Switch between the **Thumbnails**, **Tiles**, **Icons**, **List**, **Details**, **Properties**, and **Preview** views.	ALT+5
Display a shortcut menu for the selected folder or file.	SHIFT+F10
Open the **Look in** or **Save in** list (known as the **Address bar** in Windows Vista).	F4
Update the folder and file list in the **Open**, **Open in Design Mode**, or **Save As** dialog box.	F5

Use edit boxes within dialog boxes

An edit box is a field into which you can type or paste an entry, such as your user name or the path of a folder.

TASK	SHORTCUT
Move to the beginning of the entry.	HOME
Move to the end of the entry.	END
Move one character to the left.	LEFT ARROW
Move one character to the right.	RIGHT ARROW
Move one word to the left.	CTRL+LEFT ARROW
Move one word to the right.	CTRL+RIGHT ARROW
Select or cancel the selection one character to the left.	SHIFT+LEFT ARROW
Select or cancel the selection one character to the right.	SHIFT+RIGHT ARROW
Select or cancel the selection one word to the left.	CTRL+SHIFT+LEFT ARROW
Select or cancel the selection one word to the right.	CTRL+SHIFT+RIGHT ARROW
Select from the cursor to the beginning of the entry.	SHIFT+HOME
Select from the cursor to the end of the entry.	SHIFT+END

CHAPTER 11.

Keyboard Shortcuts In PowerPoint 2013.

Definition of Program: Microsoft PowerPoint is a Microsoft Corporation program designed in 1990 used for graphic presentation.

The following list of shortcut keys will help you to excel in Microsoft PowerPoint.

Use Keyboard Shortcuts To Create Your Presentation.

Frequently Used Shortcuts

The following table itemizes the most frequently used shortcuts in PowerPoint.

TASK	SHORTCUT
Make selected text bold.	Ctrl+B
Change the font size for selected text.	Alt+H, F, and then S
Change the zoom for the slide.	Alt+W, Q
Cut selected text, object, or slide.	Ctrl+X
Copy selected text, object, or slide.	Ctrl+C
Paste cut or copied text, object, or slide.	Ctrl+V
Undo the last action.	Ctrl+Z
Save the presentation.	Ctrl+S

Insert a picture.	Alt+N, P
Insert a shape.	Alt+H, S, and then H
Select a theme.	Alt+G, H
Select a slide layout.	Alt+H, L
Go to the next slide.	Page Down
Go to the previous slide.	Page Up
Go to the Home tab.	Alt+H
Move to the Insert tab.	Alt+N
Start the slide show.	Alt+S,B
End the slide show.	Esc
Close PowerPoint.	Alt+F, X

Navigate The Ribbon With Only The Keyboard

The ribbon is the strip at the top of PowerPoint, organized by tabs. Each tab displays a different ribbon, which is made up of groups, and each group includes one or more commands.

You can navigate the ribbon with just the keyboard. Access keys are special shortcuts that let you quickly use a command on the ribbon by pressing a few keys, regardless of where you are in PowerPoint. Every command in PowerPoint can be accessed by using an access key.

There are two ways to navigate the tabs in the ribbon:

- To get to the ribbon, press Alt, and then, to move between tabs, use the Right Arrow and Left Arrow keys.
- To go directly to a tab on the ribbon, press one of the following access keys:

TASK	SHORTCUT
Open the File page.	Alt+F
Open the Home tab.	Alt+H
Open the Insert tab.	Alt+N
Open the Design tab.	Alt+G
Open the Transitions tab.	Alt+T
Open the Animations tab.	Alt+A
Open the Slide Show tab.	Alt+S
Open the Review tab.	Alt+R
Open the View tab.	Alt+W
Open the Tell me box.	Alt+Q, and then enter the search term

Note: Add-ins and other programs may add new tabs to the ribbon and may provide access keys for those tabs.

Work in ribbon tabs with the keyboard

- To move to the list of ribbon tabs, press Alt; to go directly to a tab, press a keyboard shortcut.
- To move between commands, press the Tab key or Shift+Tab. You move forward or backward through the commands in order. You can also press the arrow keys.
- Controls are activated in different ways, depending upon the type of control:
  - If the selected command is a button, to activate it, press Spacebar or Enter.
  - If the selected command is a split button (that is, a button that opens a menu of additional options), to activate it, press Alt+Down Arrow. Tab through the options. To select the current option, press Spacebar or Enter.

- If the selected command is a list (such as the Font list), to open the list, press the Down Arrow key. Then, to move between items, press the arrow keys. When the item you want is selected, press Enter.
- If the selected command is a gallery, to select the command, press the Spacebar or Enter. Then, tab through the items.

Tip: In galleries with more than one row of items, the Tab key moves from the beginning to the end of the current row and, when it reaches the end of the row, it moves to the beginning of the next one. Pressing the Right Arrow key at the end of the current row moves back to the beginning of the current row.

Change Focus By Using The Keyboard

The following table lists some ways to move the focus using the keyboard.

TASK	SHORTCUT
Select the active tab of the ribbon and activate the access keys.	Alt or F10. To move to a different tab, use access keys or the arrow keys.
Move the focus to commands on the ribbon.	Tab key or Shift+Tab
Move down, up, left, or right, respectively, among the items on the ribbon.	Down Arrow, Up Arrow, Left Arrow, or Right Arrow key
Expand or collapse the ribbon.	Ctrl+F1
Display the context menu for the selected item.	Shift+F10
Move the focus to a different pane.	F6

Move to the next or previous command on the ribbon.	Tab key or Shift+Tab
Activate the selected command or control on the ribbon.	Spacebar or Enter
Open the selected menu or gallery on the ribbon.	Spacebar or Enter
Open the selected list on the ribbon, such as the Font list.	Down Arrow key
Move between items in an opened menu or gallery.	Tab key
Finish modifying a value in a control on the ribbon, and move the focus back to the document.	Enter

Use access keys when you can see the Key Tips

In PowerPoint 2013 and later, you can use Key Tips to get to things on the ribbon. You can display Key Tips, which are the letters used to access commands, and then use them to navigate in the ribbon.

1. Press Alt. The Key Tips appear in small squares by each ribbon command.
2. To select a command, press the letter shown in the square Key Tip that appears by it. For example, press F to open the **File** Tab; H to open the **Home** Tab; N to open the **Insert** Tab, and so on.

Depending on which letter you press, you may be shown additional Key Tips. For example, if you press Alt+F, Backstage view opens on the **Info** page, which has a different set of Key Tips.

Move Between Panes

TASK	SHORTCUT
Move clockwise among panes in Normal view.	F6
Move counterclockwise among panes in Normal view.	Shift+F6
Switch between the Thumbnail pane and the Outline View pane.	Ctrl+Shift+Tab

Work In An Outline

TASK	SHORTCUT
Promote a paragraph.	Alt+Shift+Left Arrow
Demote a paragraph.	Alt+Shift+Right Arrow
Move selected paragraphs up.	Alt+Shift+Up Arrow
Move selected paragraphs down.	Alt+Shift+Down Arrow
Show heading level 1	Alt+Shift+1
Expand text below a heading.	Alt+Shift+Plus Sign (+)
Collapse text below a heading.	Alt+Shift+Minus Sign (-)

Work With Shapes, Pictures, Boxes, Objects, And WordArt.

Insert a shape

1. To select **Shapes**, press Alt+N, S, and then H.
2. Use the arrow keys to move through the categories of shapes, and select the shape you want.
3. Press Ctrl+Enter to insert the shape.

Insert a text box

1. Press Alt+N, X.
2. Press Ctrl+Enter to insert the text box.

Insert an object

1. To select **Object**, press Alt+N, and J .
2. To move the focus to the **Object type** list, press Tab.
3. Press Ctrl+Enter to insert the object.

Insert WordArt

1. To select **WordArt**, press Alt+N, W .
2. Use the arrow keys to select the WordArt style you want, and press Enter.
3. Type your text.

Select a shape

Note: If your cursor is within text, press Esc before using this shortcut.

- To select a single shape, press the Tab key to cycle forward (or Shift+Tab to cycle backward) through the objects until sizing handles appear on the object you want.

Group or ungroup shapes, pictures, and WordArt objects

- To group shapes, pictures, or WordArt objects, select the items that you want to group, and press Ctrl+G.
- To ungroup a group, select the group, and press Ctrl+Shift+G.

Copy the attributes of a shape

1. Select the shape with the attributes you want to copy.

   Note: If you select a shape with text, you copy the look and style of the text in addition to the attributes of the shape.

2. To copy the object attributes, press Ctrl+Shift+C.
3. To select the object you want to copy the attributes to, press the Tab key or Shift+Tab .
4. To paste the attributes of the shape to the selected object, press Ctrl+Shift+V.

Select And Edit Text And Objects

Select text and objects

TASK	SHORTCUT
Select one character to the right.	Shift+Right Arrow
Select one character to the left.	Shift+Left Arrow
Select to the end of a word.	Ctrl+Shift+Right Arrow
Select to the beginning of a word.	Ctrl+Shift+Left Arrow
Select one line up (with the cursor at the beginning of a line).	Shift+Up Arrow
Select one line down (with the cursor at the beginning of a line).	Shift+Down Arrow
Select an object (when the text inside the object is selected).	ESC

Select another object (when one object is selected).	Tab or Shift+Tab until the object you want is selected
Send object back one position.	Ctrl+Shift+[
Send object forward one position.	Ctrl+Shift+]
Select text within an object (with an object selected).	Enter
Select all objects.	Ctrl+A (on the **Slides** tab)
Play or pause media.	Ctrl+SPACE
Select all slides.	Ctrl+A (in **Slide Sorter** view)
Select all text.	Ctrl+A (on the **Outline** tab)

Delete and copy text and objects

TASK	SHORTCUT
Delete one character to the left.	Backspace
Delete one word to the left.	Ctrl+Backspace
Delete one character to the right.	Delete
Delete one word to the right. **Note:** The cursor must be between words to do this.	Ctrl+Delete
Cut selected object or text.	Ctrl+X
Copy selected object or text.	Ctrl+C
Paste cut or copied object or text.	Ctrl+V
Undo the last action.	Ctrl+Z
Redo the last action.	Ctrl+Y
Copy formatting only.	Ctrl+Shift+C
Paste formatting only.	Ctrl+Shift+V
Copy animation painter	Alt+Shift+C
Paste animation painter	Alt+Shift+V

Open **Paste Special** dialog box.	Ctrl+Alt+V

Move around in text

TASK	SHORTCUT
Move one character to the left.	Left Arrow
Move one character to the right.	Right Arrow
Move one line up.	Up Arrow
Move one line down.	Down Arrow
Move one word to the left.	Ctrl+Left Arrow
Move one word to the right.	Ctrl+Right Arrow
Move to the end of a line.	End
Move to the beginning of a line.	Home
Move up one paragraph.	Ctrl+Up Arrow
Move down one paragraph.	Ctrl+Down Arrow
Move to the end of a text box.	Ctrl+End
Move to the beginning of a text box.	Ctrl+Home
Move to the next title or body text placeholder. If it is the last placeholder on a slide, this action inserts a new slide with the same slide layout as the original slide.	Ctrl+Enter
Move to repeat the last **Find** action.	Shift+F4

Move around in and work in tables

TASK	SHORTCUT
Move to the next cell.	Tab
Move to the preceding cell.	Shift+Tab
Move to the next row.	Down Arrow
Move to the preceding row.	Up Arrow

Insert a tab in a cell.	Ctrl+Tab
Start a new paragraph.	Enter
Add a new row at the bottom of the table.	Tab in the bottom right table cell.

Edit a linked or embedded object

1. To select the object you want, press Tab or Shift+Tab.
2. To open the shortcut menu, press Shift+F10.
3. To select **Worksheet Object**, press the Down Arrow key until it's selected.
4. To select **Edit**, press the Right Arrow key and then press Enter.

Note: The name of the command in the shortcut menu depends on the type of embedded or linked object. For example, an embedded Microsoft Office Excel worksheet has the command **Worksheet Object**, whereas an embedded Microsoft Office Visio Drawing has the command **Visio Object**.

Format Text

Note: Select the text you want to change before using these keyboard shortcuts.

Change or resize a font

TASK	SHORTCUT
Open the **Font** dialog box to change the font.	Ctrl+Shift+F
Increase the font size.	Ctrl+Shift+Right Angle bracket (>)
Decrease the font size.	Ctrl+Shift+Left Angle bracket (<)

Apply character formatting

TASK	SHORTCUT
Open the **Font** dialog box to change the formatting of characters.	Ctrl+T
Change between sentence case, lowercase, or uppercase.	Shift+F3
Apply bold formatting.	Ctrl+B
Apply an underline.	Ctrl+U
Apply italic formatting.	Ctrl+I
Apply subscript formatting (automatic spacing).	Ctrl+Equal sign (=)
Apply superscript formatting (automatic spacing).	Ctrl+Shift+Plus sign (+)
Remove manual character formatting, such as subscript and superscript.	Ctrl+Spacebar
Insert a hyperlink.	Ctrl+K

Copy text formatting

TASK	SHORTCUT
Copy formats.	Ctrl+Shift+C
Paste formats.	Ctrl+Shift+V

Align paragraphs

TASK	SHORTCUT
Center a paragraph.	Ctrl+E
Justify a paragraph.	Ctrl+J
Left align a paragraph.	Ctrl+L
Right align a paragraph.	Ctrl+R

Custom Keyboard Shortcuts

To assign custom keyboard shortcuts to menu items, recorded macros, and Visual Basic for Applications (VBA) code in PowerPoint, you must use a third-party add-in, such as Shortcut Manager for PowerPoint, which is available from OfficeOne Add-Ins for PowerPoint.

Use Keyboard Shortcuts To Deliver Your Presentation.

This topic itemizes keyboard shortcuts for delivering your presentation in PowerPoint 2016.

- The shortcuts in this topic refer to the US keyboard layout. Keys for other layouts might not correspond exactly to the keys on a US keyboard.
- If a shortcut requires pressing two or more keys at the same time, this topic separates the keys with a plus sign (+). If you have to press one key immediately after another, the keys are separated by a comma (,).

Note: This topic assumes that JAWS users have turned off the Virtual Ribbon Menu feature.

Control Your Slide Show During The Presentation.

The following keyboard shortcuts apply while you're delivering your presentation in Slide Show (full-screen) mode. To enter **Slide Show** mode, press Alt+S, B.

TASK	SHORTCUT

Perform the next animation or advance to the next slide.	N, Enter, Page Down, Right Arrow, Down Arrow, or Spacebar
Perform the previous animation or return to the previous slide.	P, Page Up, Left Arrow, Up Arrow, or Backspace
Go to slide number.	number+Enter
Display a blank black slide, or return to the presentation from a blank black slide.	B or Period
Display a blank white slide, or return to the presentation from a blank white slide.	W or Comma
Stop or restart an automatic presentation.	S
End a presentation.	ESC
Erase on-screen annotations.	E
Go to the next slide, if the next slide is hidden.	H
Set new timings while rehearsing.	T
Re-record slide narration and timing	R
Return to the first slide.	Press and hold Left Mouse button for several seconds
Change the pointer to a pen.	Ctrl+P
Change the pointer to an arrow.	Ctrl+A
Change the pointer to an eraser	Ctrl+E
Show or hide ink markup	Ctrl+M
Hide the pointer and navigation button immediately.	Ctrl+H

Hide the pointer and navigation button in 15 seconds.	Ctrl+U
View the **All Slides** dialog box	Ctrl+S
View the computer task bar	Ctrl+T
Display the shortcut menu.	Shift+F10
Go to the first or next hyperlink on the current slide.	Tab
Go to the last or previous hyperlink on the current slide.	Shift+Tab
Perform the "mouse click" behavior of the selected hyperlink. (Follow a selected hyperlink)	Enter while a hyperlink is selected

Control Video And Other Media During A Presentation.

These keyboard shortcuts work with video files imported from your computer or other device. They don't work with online video files.

During your presentation, if you want to see the list of media shortcuts, press F1. Then, in the **Slide Show Help** dialog box, go to the **Media** tab.

TASK	SHORTCUT
Stop media playback.	Alt+Q
Play or pause media.	Ctrl+Space
Toggle between play and pause.	Alt+P
Go to the next bookmark.	Alt+End
Go to the previous bookmark.	Alt+Home

Increase the sound volume.	Alt+Up
Decrease the sound volume.	Alt+Down
Seek forward.	Alt+Shift+Page Down
Seek backward.	Alt+Shift+Page Up
Mute the sound.	Alt+U

CHAPTER 12.

Keyboard Shortcuts In Visio 2013.

Definition of Program: Microsoft Visio is a diagramming and vector graphics application that was acquired by Microsoft in 2000. With Microsoft Visio, diagrams can be created with just a few clicks.

The following list of shortcut keys will help you to excel in Microsoft Visio.

Visio-Specific Tasks

Format text

TASK	SHORTCUT
Open the **Home** tab in the ribbon	ALT+H
Open the **Text** dialog box.	F11
Open the **Format Shape** task pane.	F3

Use the Snap & Glue features

TASK	SHORTCUT
Open the **Snap & Glue** dialog box.	ALT+F9

Group, rotate, and flip shapes

TASK	SHORTCUT
Group the selected shapes.	CTRL+G or CTRL+SHIFT+G

Ungroup shapes in the selected group.	CTRL+SHIFT+U
Bring the selected shape to the front.	CTRL+SHIFT+F
Send the selected shape to the back.	CTRL+SHIFT+B
Rotate the selected shape to the left.	CTRL+L
Rotate the selected shape to the right.	CTRL+R
Flip the selected shape horizontally.	CTRL+H
Flip the selected shape vertically.	CTRL+J
Open the **Align Shapes** dialog box for the selected shape.	F8

View drawing windows

TASK	SHORTCUT
Display the open drawing windows tiled vertically.	SHIFT+F7
Display the open drawing windows tiled horizontally.	CTRL+SHIFT+F7
Display the open drawing windows so that you can see the title of every window.	ALT+F7 or CTRL+ALT+F7

Visio-Specific Toolbars

Select tools

TASK	SHORTCUT
Switch the **Format Painter** tool on or off ().	CTRL+SHIFT+P

Select the **Pointer Tool** ( ).	CTRL+1
Select the **Connector** tool ( ).	CTRL+3
Select the connection point tool	CTRL+SHIFT+1
Select the text tool (**A**).	CTRL+2
Select the text box tool ( ).	CTRL+SHIFT+4

Select the drawing tools

TASK	SHORTCUT
Select the **Rectangle Tool** (□).	CTRL+8
Select the **Ellipse Tool** (○).	CTRL+9
Select the **Line Tool** ( ).	CTRL+6
Select the **Arc Tool** ( ).	CTRL+7
Select the **Freeform Tool** ( ).	CTRL+5
Select the **Pencil Tool** ( ).	CTRL+4

Crop a picture

TASK	SHORTCUT
Select the **Crop** tool ( ).	CTRL+SHIFT+2

Visio Shapes And Stencils

Move from shape to shape in a drawing page

TASK	SHORTCUT
Move from shape to shape on the drawing page. A dotted rectangle indicates the shape that has the focus. **Note:** You cannot move to shapes that are protected against selection or on a locked layer.	TAB
Move from shape to shape on the drawing page in reverse order.	SHIFT+TAB

Select a shape that has focus. **Note:** To select multiple shapes, press the TAB key to bring focus to the first shape you want to select, and then press ENTER. Hold down SHIFT while you press the TAB key to bring focus to another shape. When the focus rectangle is over the shape you want, press ENTER to add that shape to the selection. Repeat for each shape you want to select.	ENTER
Clear selection of or focus on a shape.	ESC
Switch between text edit mode and shape selection mode on a selected shape.	F2
Nudge a selected shape.	Arrow keys
Nudge a selected shape 1 pixel at a time. **Note:** SCROLL LOCK must be turned off.	SHIFT+Arrow keys

Work with master shapes in a stencil

TASK	SHORTCUT
Move between master shapes in a stencil.	Arrow keys
Move to the first master shape in a row of a stencil.	HOME
Move to the last master shape in a row of a stencil.	END
Move to the first master shape in a column of a stencil.	PAGE UP
Move to the last master shape in a column of a stencil.	PAGE DOWN

Copy the selected master shapes to the Clipboard.	CTRL+C
Paste the contents of the Clipboard to a new stencil. **Note:** The new stencil must first be opened for editing.	CTRL+V
Select all the master shapes in a stencil. **Note:** To select multiple master shapes (instead of all), press the arrow keys to bring focus to the first master shape you want. Hold down SHIFT while you press the arrow keys to bring focus to another master shape. When the focus rectangle is over the shape that you want, press ENTER to add that shape to the selection. Repeat for each shape that you want to select.	CTRL+A
Select or cancel selection of a master shape that has focus.	SHIFT+ENTER
Cancel the selection of master shapes in a stencil.	ESC
Insert the selected master shapes into the drawing.	CTRL+ENTER

Work with stencils in edit mode

TASK	SHORTCUT
Delete the selected master shape.	DELETE
Cut the selected master shape from the custom stencil and put it on the Clipboard.	CTRL+X
Rename the selected master shape.	F2

Online Help

Keyboard shortcuts for using the Help window

The Help window provides access to all Office Help content. The Help window displays topics and other Help content.

In the Help window

TASK	SHORTCUT
Open the Help window.	F1
Close the Help window.	ALT+F4
Switch between the Help window and the active program.	ALT+TAB
Go back to Visio Help Home.	ALT+HOME
Select the next item in the Help window.	TAB
Select the previous item in the Help window.	SHIFT+TAB
Perform the action for the selected item.	ENTER
Select the next hidden text or hyperlink, including **Show All** or **Hide All** at the top of a topic.	TAB
Select the previous hidden text or hyperlink.	SHIFT+TAB
Perform the action for the selected **Show All**, **Hide All**, hidden text, or hyperlink.	ENTER
Move back to the previous Help topic (**Back** button).	ALT+LEFT ARROW
Move forward to the next Help topic (**Forward** button).	ALT+RIGHT ARROW

Scroll small amounts up or down, respectively, within the currently displayed Help topic.	UP ARROW or DOWN ARROW
Scroll larger amounts up or down, respectively, within the currently displayed Help topic.	PAGE UP or PAGE DOWN

Microsoft Office basics

Display and use windows

TASK	SHORTCUT
Switch to the next window.	ALT+TAB
Close the active window.	ALT+F4
Move to a task pane from another pane in the program window (clockwise direction). You may need to press F6 more than once. **Note:** If pressing F6 does not display the task pane you want, try pressing ALT to put focus on the ribbon.	F6
Maximize a selected window.	CTRL+F10
Restore the size of the Visio program window after you maximized it.	CTRL+F5
Copy a picture of the screen to the Clipboard.	PRINT SCREEN
Copy a picture of the selected window to the Clipboard.	ALT+PRINT SCREEN
For any window with an icon in its title bar (for example, a shapes window), display the window shortcut menu.	ALT+SPACEBAR

Open the **Page** dialog box.	SHIFT+F4
Open the **Reorder Pages** dialog box.	CTRL+ALT+P
Cycle the focus through open drawings.	CTRL+TAB or CTRL+F6
Cycle the focus through open drawings in reverse order.	CTRL+SHIFT+TAB or CTRL+SHIFT+F6
Cycle the focus through pages in a drawing, including any visible markup overlays.	CTRL+PAGE DOWN
Cycle the focus through pages in a drawing in reverse order.	CTRL+PAGE UP
When a task pane is active, select the next or previous option in the task pane.	TAB or SHIFT+TAB

Change or resize the font

TASK	SHORTCUT
Increase the font size of the selected text.	CTRL+SHIFT+>
Decrease the font size of the selected text.	CTRL+SHIFT+<

Move around in text or cells

TASK	SHORTCUT
Move one character to the left.	LEFT ARROW
Move one character to the right.	RIGHT ARROW
Move one line up.	UP ARROW
Move one line down.	DOWN ARROW
Move one word to the left.	CTRL+LEFT ARROW
Move one word to the right.	CTRL+RIGHT ARROW
Move to the end of a line.	END

Move to the beginning of a line.	HOME
Move up one paragraph.	CTRL+UP ARROW
Move down one paragraph.	CTRL+DOWN ARROW
Move to the end of a text box.	CTRL+END
Move to the beginning of a text box.	CTRL+HOME

Access and use task panes

TASK	SHORTCUT
Move to a task pane from another pane in the program window. (You may need to press F6 more than once.) **Note:** If pressing F6 does not display the task pane you want, try pressing ALT to put the focus on the ribbon and then pressing F6 to move to the task pane.	F6
When a task pane is active, select the next or previous option in the task pane.	TAB or SHIFT+TAB
Move among choices on a selected submenu; move among certain options in a group of options in a dialog box.	DOWN ARROW or UP ARROW
Open the selected menu, or perform the action assigned to the selected button.	SPACEBAR or ENTER
Open a shortcut menu	SHIFT+F10
When a menu or submenu is visible, select the first or last command,	HOME or END

respectively, on the menu or submenu.	

Float or anchor task panes

1. Press F6 repeatedly to select the task pane that you want.
2. Press ALT+SPACEBAR to open the menu for that task pane.
3. Press the DOWN ARROW key to select the **Float Window** command, and then press ENTER.

Use dialog boxes

TASK	SHORTCUT
Move to the next option or option group.	TAB
Move to the previous option or option group.	SHIFT+TAB
Switch to the next tab in a dialog box.	CTRL+TAB
Switch to the previous tab in a dialog box.	CTRL+SHIFT+TAB
Move between options in an open drop-down list, or between options in a group of options.	Arrow keys
Perform the action assigned to the selected button; select or clear the selected check box.	SPACEBAR
Open the list if it is closed and move to that option in the list.	First letter of an option in a drop-down list
Select an option; select or clear a check box.	ALT+ the letter underlined in an option

Open a selected drop-down list.	ALT+DOWN ARROW
Close a selected drop-down list; cancel a command and close a dialog box.	ESC
Perform the action assigned to a default button in a dialog box.	ENTER

Use edit boxes within dialog boxes

An edit box is a blank in which you type or paste an entry, such as your user name or the path of a folder.

TASK	SHORTCUT
Move to the beginning of the entry.	HOME
Move to the end of the entry.	END
Move one character to the left or right.	LEFT ARROW or RIGHT ARROW
Move one word to the left.	CTRL+LEFT ARROW
Move one word to the right.	CTRL+RIGHT ARROW
Select or cancel selection one character to the left.	SHIFT+LEFT ARROW
Select or cancel selection one character to the right.	SHIFT+RIGHT ARROW
Select or cancel selection one word to the left.	CTRL+SHIFT+LEFT ARROW
Select or cancel selection one word to the right.	CTRL+SHIFT+RIGHT ARROW
Select from the insertion point to the beginning of the entry.	SHIFT+HOME

Select from the insertion point to the end of the entry.	SHIFT+END

Use the Open and Save As dialog boxes

TASK	SHORTCUT
Move to the next option or option group.	TAB
Move to the previous option or option group.	SHIFT+TAB
Move between options in an open drop-down list, or between options in a group of options.	Arrow keys
Perform the action assigned to the selected button	ENTER, SPACEBAR
Move to the **Save as type** list in the **Save As** dialog box	ALT+T
Move to the **File name** box	ALT+N
Move to the file type list in the **Open** dialog box	ALT+T
Open a selected file in the **Open** dialog box	ALT+O
Save the current file in the **Save** dialog box	ALT+S
Open a selected drop-down list.	ALT+DOWN ARROW
Close a selected drop-down list; cancel a command and close a dialog box.	ESC
Update the file list	F5
Display a shortcut menu for a selected item such as a folder or file	SHIFT+F10

Text

Edit text

TASK	SHORTCUT
Move to the next or previous character, respectively, in a line of text.	RIGHT ARROW or LEFT ARROW
Move to the next or previous line of text, respectively.	DOWN ARROW or UP ARROW
Move to the next or previous word, respectively, in a line of text.	CTRL+RIGHT ARROW or CTRL+LEFT ARROW
Move to the next or previous paragraph, respectively.	CTRL+DOWN ARROW or CTRL+UP ARROW
Select all the text in a text block.	CTRL+A
Select the next or previous character, respectively.	SHIFT+RIGHT ARROW or SHIFT+LEFT ARROW
Select the next or previous word, respectively.	CTRL+SHIFT+RIGHT ARROW or CTRL+SHIFT+LEFT ARROW
Select the next or previous line, respectively.	SHIFT+DOWN ARROW or SHIFT+UP ARROW
Select the next or previous paragraph, respectively.	CTRL+SHIFT+DOWN ARROW or CTRL+SHIFT+UP ARROW
Delete the previous word.	CTRL+BACKSPACE
Replace the selected text with the field height. If no	CTRL+SHIFT+H

text is selected, replace all text with the field height for the selected shape.	

Format text

TASK	SHORTCUT
Turn bold (**B**) on or off.	CTRL+B
Turn italic (*I*) on or off.	CTRL+I
Turn underline (U) on or off.	CTRL+U
Turn double underline on or off.	CTRL+SHIFT+D
Turn all caps on or off.	CTRL+SHIFT+A
Turn small caps on or off.	CTRL+SHIFT+K
Turn subscript (x_2) on or off.	CTRL+=
Turn superscript (x^2) on or off.	CTRL+SHIFT+=
Increase the font size of the selected text.	CTRL+SHIFT+>
Decrease the font size of the selected text.	CTRL+SHIFT+<

Align text

TASK	SHORTCUT
Align text left.	CTRL+SHIFT+L
Center text horizontally.	CTRL+SHIFT+C
Align text right.	CTRL+SHIFT+R
Justify text horizontally.	CTRL+SHIFT+J
Top-align text vertically.	CTRL+SHIFT+T
Center text vertically.	CTRL+SHIFT+M
Bottom-align text vertically.	CTRL+SHIFT+V

Zoom and Navigation

Navigate the Ribbon

1. Press ALT.

   The KeyTips are displayed over each feature that is available in the current view.

2. Press the letter shown in the KeyTip over the feature that you want to use.
3. Depending on which letter you press, you may be shown additional KeyTips. For example, if the **Home** tab is active and you press N, the **Insert** tab is displayed, along with the KeyTips for the groups on that tab.
4. Continue pressing letters until you press the letter of the command or control that you want to use. In some cases, you must first press the letter of the group that contains the command. For example, if the **Home** tab is active, press ALT+H, F, S will take you to the **Size** list box in the **Font** group.

   Note: To cancel the action that you are taking and hide the KeyTips, press ALT.

Zoom

TASK	SHORTCUT
Zoom in.	ALT+F6
Zoom out.	ALT+SHIFT+F6
Fit to window	CTRL+SHIFT+W

Move Around in Full-screen View

Use these keyboard shortcuts to move between Visio and another program or page when you are in full-screen view.

TASK	SHORTCUT
Enter full-screen view	F5
Exit full-screen view	ESC
Open the next page in the drawing.	PAGE DOWN
Return to the previous page in the drawing.	PAGE UP

Move Around a Web page Drawing

TASK	SHORTCUT
Cycle the focus through the left frame, the drawing, and shapes on the drawing that contain shape data, hyperlinks, and the address bar.	TAB
Activate the hyperlink for the shape or hyperlink on the drawing that has focus.	ENTER

CHAPTER 13.

Keyboard Shortcuts In Project 2013.

Definition of Program: Microsoft Project is a project management software, developed and sold by Microsoft that helps users to create schedules, distribute resources and manage budgets.

The following list of shortcut keys will help you to excel in Microsoft Project.

Microsoft Office Basics

Keyboard Access to the Ribbon

1. Press Alt.
   The KeyTips are displayed over each feature that is available in the current view.
2. Press the letter that appears in the KeyTip over the feature that you want to use.
3. Depending on which letter you press, additional KeyTips may appear. For example, if the **Home** tab is active and you press W, the **View** tab is displayed, along with the KeyTips for the groups on that tab.
4. Continue pressing letters until you press the letter of the command or control that you want to use. In some cases, you must first press the letter of the group that contains the command.

   Note: To cancel the action that you are taking and hide the KeyTips, press Alt.

Display And Use Windows

TASK	SHORTCUT
Switch to the next window.	Alt+Tab
Switch to the previous window.	Alt+Shift+Tab
Close the active window.	Ctrl+W or Ctrl+F4
Restore the size of the active window after you maximize it.	Ctrl+F5
Move to a task pane from another pane in the program window (clockwise direction). You may need to press F6 more than once.	F6
Move to a pane from another pane in the program window (counterclockwise direction).	Shift+F6
When more than one window is open, switch to the next window.	Ctrl+F6
Switch to the previous window.	Ctrl+Shift+F6
Maximize or restore a selected window.	Ctrl+F10
Copy a picture of the screen to the Clipboard.	Print Screen
Copy a picture of the selected window to the Clipboard.	Alt+Print Screen

Move Around in Text or Cells

TASK	SHORTCUT
Move one character to the left.	Left Arrow
Move one character to the right.	Right Arrow
Move one line up.	Up Arrow
Move one line down.	Down Arrow
Move one word to the left.	Ctrl+Left Arrow
Move one word to the right.	Ctrl+Right Arrow
Move to the end of a line.	End

Move to the beginning of a line.	Home
Move up one paragraph.	Ctrl+Up Arrow
Move down one paragraph.	Ctrl+Down Arrow
Move to the end of a text box.	Ctrl+End
Move to the beginning of a text box.	Ctrl+Home

Move Around in and Work in Tables

TASK	SHORTCUT
Move to the next cell.	Tab
Move to the preceding cell.	Shift+Tab
Move to the next row.	Down Arrow
Move to the preceding row.	Up Arrow
Insert a tab in a cell.	Ctrl+Tab
Start a new paragraph.	Enter
Add a new row at the bottom of the table.	Tab at the end of the last row

Access and Use Actions

TASK	SHORTCUT
Display the menu or message for an action. If more than one action is present, switch to the next action and display its menu or message.	Alt+Shift+F10
Select the next item on the action menu.	Down Arrow
Select the previous item on the action menu.	Up Arrow
Perform the action for the selected item on the action menu.	Enter
Close the action menu or message.	Esc

Tips

- You can ask to be notified by a sound whenever an action appears. To hear audio cues, you must have a sound card. You must also have Microsoft Office Sounds installed on your computer.
- You can download Microsoft Office Sounds from Office.com.

Use Dialog Boxes

TASK	SHORTCUT
Move to the next option or option group.	Tab
Move to the previous option or option group.	Shift+Tab
Switch to the next tab in a dialog box.	Ctrl+Tab
Switch to the previous tab in a dialog box.	Ctrl+Shift+Tab
Move between options in an open drop-down list, or between options in a group of options.	Arrow keys
Perform the action assigned to the selected button; select or clear the selected check box.	Insert
Open the list if it is closed and move to that option in the list.	First letter of an option in a drop-down list
Select an option; select or clear a check box.	Alt+ the letter underlined in an option
Open a selected drop-down list.	Alt+Down Arrow

Close a selected drop-down list; cancel a command and close a dialog box.	Esc
Perform the action assigned to a default button in a dialog box.	Enter

Use Edit Boxes Within Dialog Boxes

An edit box is a blank in which you type or paste an entry, such as your user name or the path to a folder.

TASK	SHORTCUT
Move to the beginning of the entry.	Home
Move to the end of the entry.	End
Move one character to the left or right, respectively.	Left Arrow or Right Arrow
Move one word to the left.	Ctrl+Left Arrow
Move one word to the right.	Ctrl+Right Arrow
Select or cancel selection one character to the left.	Shift+Left Arrow
Select or cancel selection one character to the right.	Shift+Right Arrow
Select or cancel selection one word to the left.	Ctrl+Shift+Left Arrow
Select or cancel selection one word to the right.	Ctrl+Shift+Right Arrow
Select from the insertion point to the beginning of the entry.	Shift+Home
Select from the insertion point to the end of the entry.	Shift+End

Basic File Management

TASK	SHORTCUT
Open a project file (display the **Open** dialog box).	Ctrl+F12
Open a project file (display the **Open** tab in the Backstage view).	Ctrl+O
Save a project file.	Ctrl+S
Create a new project.	Ctrl+N
Print a file (display the **Print** tab in the Backstage view).	Ctrl+P

Use the Open and Save As Dialog Boxes

TASK	SHORTCUT
Display the **Open** dialog box.	Ctrl+F12
Display the **Open** tab in the Backstage view.	Ctrl+O
Display the **Save As** dialog box.	F12
Open the selected folder or file.	Enter
Open the folder one level above the open folder.	Backspace
Delete the selected folder or file.	Delete
Display a shortcut menu for a selected item such as a folder or file.	Shift+F10
Move forward through options	Tab
Move back through options	Shift+Tab
Open the **Look in** list	F4 or Alt+1

Microsoft Project Quick Reference

Use a Network Diagram

TASK	SHORTCUT

Move to a different Network Diagram box.	Arrow keys
Add Network Diagram boxes to the selection.	Shift+Arrow keys
Move a Network Diagram box. **Note:** You need to set manual positioning first. Select the box you want to move. Click **Format**, and then click **Layout**. Click **Allow manual box positioning**.	Ctrl+Arrow keys
Move to the top Network Diagram box in the view or project.	Ctrl+Home or Shift+Ctrl+Home
Move to the lowest Network Diagram box in the project.	Ctrl+End or Shift+Ctrl+End
Move to the leftmost Network Diagram box in the project.	Home or Shift+Home
Move to the rightmost Network Diagram box in the project.	End or Shift+End
Move up one window height.	Page Up or Shift+Page Up
Move down one window height.	Page Down or Shift+Page Down
Move left one window width.	Ctrl+Page Up or Shift+Ctrl+Page Up
Move right one window width.	Ctrl+Page Down or Shift+Ctrl+Page Down
Select the next field in the Network Diagram box.	Enter or Tab
Select the previous field in the Network Diagram box.	Shift+Enter

Use OfficeArt objects.

Move OfficeArt shapes.

TASK	SHORTCUT
Nudge the shape up, down, right, or left.	Arrow keys
Increase the shape's width by 10%.	Shift+Right Arrow
Decrease the shape's width by 10%.	Shift+Left Arrow
Increase the shape's height by 10%.	Shift+Up Arrow
Decrease the shape's height by 10%.	Shift+Down Arrow
Increase the shape's width by 1%.	Ctrl+Shift+Right Arrow
Decrease the shape's width by 1%.	Ctrl+Shift+Left Arrow
Increase the shape's height by 1%.	Ctrl+Shift+Up Arrow
Decrease the shape's height by 1%.	Ctrl+Shift+Down Arrow
Rotate the shape 15 degrees to the right.	Alt+Right Arrow
Rotate the shape 15 degrees to the left.	Alt+Left Arrow

Select and copy OfficeArt objects and text

TASK	SHORTCUT
Select an object (with text selected inside the object).	Esc

Select an object (with an object selected).	Tab or Shift+Tab until the object you want is selected
Select text within an object (with an object selected).	Enter
Select multiple shapes	Press and hold Ctrl while you click the shapes
Select multiple shapes with text	Press and hold Shift while you click the shapes
Cut selected object.	Ctrl+X
Copy selected object.	Ctrl+C
Paste cut or copied object.	Ctrl+V
Paste special.	Ctrl+Alt+V
Copy formatting only.	Ctrl+Shift+C
Paste formatting only.	Ctrl+Shift+V
Paste special.	Ctrl+Alt+V
Group shapes, pictures, or WordArt.	Ctrl+G after you select the items that you want to group
Ungroup shapes, pictures, or WordArt.	Ctrl+Shift+G after you select the group that you want to ungroup
Undo the last action.	Ctrl+Z
Redo the last action.	Ctrl+Y
Add next object to a multi-selection.	Ctrl+Click
Adds next object to a multi-selection; allows clicking on textbox text to add the textbox to the multi-selection.	Shift+Click

Edit OfficeArt text and textboxes

TASK	SHORTCUT
Collapse selection.	Esc
Select all text.	Ctrl+A
Delete one word to the left.	Ctrl+Backspace
Delete one word to the right.	Ctrl+Delete
Undo.	Ctrl+Z
Redo.	Ctrl+Y
Move one word to the left.	Ctrl+Left Arrow
Move one word to the right.	Ctrl+Right Arrow
Move to the beginning of the line.	Home
Move to the end of the line.	End
Move up one paragraph.	Ctrl+Up Arrow
Move down one paragraph.	Ctrl+Down Arrow
Move to the beginning of the object's text.	Ctrl+Home
Move to the end of the object's text	Ctrl+End

Navigate Views and Windows

TASK	SHORTCUT
Activate the entry bar to edit text in a field.	F2
Activate the menu bar.	F10 or Alt
Activate the project control menu.	Alt+Hyphen or Alt+Spacebar
Activate the split bar.	Shift+F6
Close the program window.	Alt+F4
Display all filtered tasks or all filtered resources.	F3
Display the **Field Settings** dialog box.	Alt+F3
Open a new window.	Shift+F11

Reduce a selection to a single field.	Shift+Backspace
Reset sort order to ID order and turn off grouping.	Shift+F3
Select a drawing object.	F6
Display task information.	Shift+F2
Display resource information.	Shift+F2
Display assignment information.	Shift+F2
Turn on or off the Add To Selection mode.	Shift+F8
Turn on or off Auto Calculate.	Ctrl+F9
Turn on or off the Extend Selection mode.	F8
Move left, right, up, or down to view different pages in the Print Preview window.	Alt+Arrow keys

Outline a Project

TASK	SHORTCUT
Hide subtasks.	Alt+Shift+Hyphen or Alt+Shift+Minus Sign (minus sign on the numeric keypad)
Indent the selected task.	Alt+Shift+Right Arrow
Show subtasks.	Alt+Shift+ = or Alt+Shift+Plus Sign (plus sign on the numeric keypad)
Show all tasks.	Alt+Shift+* (asterisk on the numeric keypad)
Outdent the selected task.	Alt+Shift+Left Arrow

Select and edit in a dialog box

TASK	SHORTCUT
Move between fields at the bottom of a form.	Arrow keys
Move into tables at the bottom of a form.	Alt+1 (left) or Alt+2 (right)
Move to the next task or resource.	Enter
Move to the previous task or resource.	Shift+Enter

Select and edit in a sheet view

Edit in a view

TASK	SHORTCUT
Cancel an entry.	Esc
Clear or reset the selected field.	Ctrl+Delete
Copy the selected data.	Ctrl+C
Cut the selected data.	Ctrl+X
Delete the selected data.	Delete
Delete row that has a selected cell.	Ctrl+Minus Sign (on the numeric keypad)
Fill down.	Ctrl+D
Display the **Find** dialog box.	Ctrl+F or Shift+F5
In the **Find** dialog box, continue to the next instance of the search results.	Shift+F4
Use the **Go To** command (**Edit** menu).	F5
Link tasks.	Ctrl+F2
Paste the copied or cut data.	Ctrl+V

Reduce the selection to one field.	Shift+Backspace
Undo the last action.	Ctrl+Z
Unlink tasks.	Ctrl+Shift+F2
Set the task to manually schedule	Ctrl+Shift+M
Set the task to auto schedule	Ctrl+Shift+A

Move in a View

TASK	SHORTCUT
Move to the beginning of a project (timescale).	Alt+Home
Move to the end of a project (timescale).	Alt+End
Move the timescale left.	Alt+Left Arrow
Move the timescale right.	Alt+Right Arrow
Move to the first field in a row.	Home or Ctrl+Left Arrow
Move to the first row.	Ctrl+Up Arrow
Move to the first field of the first row.	Ctrl+Home
Move to the last field in a row.	End or Ctrl+Right Arrow
Move to the last field of the last row.	Ctrl+End
Move to the last row.	Ctrl+Down Arrow

Move in the Side Pane

TASK	SHORTCUT
Move focus between the side pane and the view on the right side.	Ctrl+Tab or Ctrl+Shift+Tab
Select different controls in the side pane if focus is in the side pane.	Tab

Select or clear check boxes and option buttons if focus is in the side pane.	Spacebar

Select in a View

TASK	SHORTCUT
Extend the selection down one page.	Shift+Page Down
Extend the selection up one page.	Shift+Page Up
Extend the selection down one row.	Shift+Down Arrow
Extend the selection up one row.	Shift+Up Arrow
Extend the selection to the first field in a row.	Shift+Home
Extend the selection to the last field in a row.	Shift+End
Extend the selection to the start of the information.	Ctrl+Shift+Home
Extend the selection to the end of the information.	Ctrl+Shift+End
Extend the selection to the first row.	Ctrl+Shift+Up Arrow
Extend the selection to the last row.	Ctrl+Shift+Down Arrow
Extend the selection to the first field of the first row.	Ctrl+Shift+Home
Extend the selection to the last field of the last row.	Ctrl+Shift+End
Select all rows and columns.	Ctrl+Shift+Spacebar
Select a column.	Ctrl+Spacebar
Select a row.	Shift+Spacebar

Move within a selection down one field.	Enter
Move within a selection up one field.	Shift+Enter
Move within a selection right one field.	Tab
Move within a selection left one field.	Shift+Tab

Select and Edit in the Entry Bar

TASK	SHORTCUT
Accept an entry.	Enter
Cancel an entry.	Esc
Delete one character to the left.	Backspace
Delete one character to the right.	Delete
Delete one word to the right.	Ctrl+Delete
Extend the selection to the end of the text.	Shift+End
Extend the selection to the start of the text.	Shift+Home
Turn on or off Overtype mode.	Insert

Use a Timescale

TASK	SHORTCUT
Move the timescale left one page.	Alt+Page Up
Move the timescale right one page.	Alt+Page Down
Move the timescale to beginning of the project.	Alt+Home
Move the timescale to end of the project.	Alt+End
Scroll the timescale left.	Alt+Left Arrow

Scroll the timescale right.	Alt+Right Arrow
Show smaller time units.	Ctrl+ / (slash on the numeric keypad)
Show larger time units.	Ctrl+* (asterisk on the numeric keypad)

Customer's Page.

This page is for customers who enjoyed Office 2013 Keyboard Shortcuts For Windows.

Dearly beloved customer, please leave a review behind if you enjoyed this book or found it helpful. It will be highly appreciated, thank you.

Download Our Free EBooks Today.

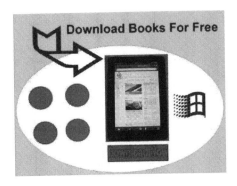

In order to appreciate our customers, we have made some of our titles available at 0.00. Totally free. Feel free to get a copy of the free titles.

(A) For Keyboard Shortcuts In Windows

Go to Amazon: <u>Windows 7 Keyboard shortcuts</u>

Go to Other Stores: <u>Windows 7 Keyboard Shortcuts</u>

(B) For Keyboard Shortcuts In Office 2016

Go to Amazon: <u>Word 2016 Keyboard Shortcuts For windows</u>

Go to Other Stores: <u>Word 2016 Keyboard Shortcuts For Windows</u>

Note: Feel free to download them from your favorite store today. Thank you!

Other Books By This Publisher.

S/N	Title	Series
Series A: Limits Breaking Quotes.		
1	Discover Your Key Christian Quotes	Limits Breaking Quotes
Series B: Shortcut Matters.		
1	Windows 7 Shortcuts	Shortcut Matters
2	Windows 7 Shortcuts & Tips	Shortcut Matters
3	Windows 8.1 Shortcuts	Shortcut Matters
4	Windows 10 Shortcut Keys	Shortcut Matters
5	Microsoft Office 2007 Keyboard Shortcuts For Windows.	Shortcut Matters
6	Microsoft Office 2010 Shortcuts For Windows.	Shortcut Matters
7	Microsoft Office 2016 Shortcuts For Windows.	Shortcut Matters
8	Microsoft Office 365/2016 Keyboard Shortcuts For Macintosh.	Shortcut Matters
Series C: Teach Yourself.		
1	Teach Yourself Computer Fundamentals	Teach Yourself
Series D: For Painless Publishing		
1	Self-Publish it with CreateSpace.	For Painless Publishing
2	Where is my money? Now solved for Kindle and CreateSpace	For Painless Publishing
3	Describe it on Amazon	For Painless Publishing
4	How To Market That Book.	For Painless Publishing

Made in the USA
Middletown, DE
25 March 2018